Cunningham's
Magical
Sampler

About the Author

Scott Cunningham practiced magic actively for over twenty years. He was the author of more than fifty books covering both fiction and non-fiction subject matter; sixteen of his titles are published by Llewellyn Publications. Scott's books reflect a broad range of interests within the New Age sphere, where he was very highly regarded. He passed from this life on March 28, 1993, after a long illness.

FOREWORD BY RAYMOND BUCKLAND

Cunningham's
Magical
Sampler

*Collected
Writings and Spells
from the Renowned
Wiccan Author*

Llewellyn Worldwide
Woodbury, Minnesota

First Edition
Second Printing, 2013

Book design by Bob Gaul
Cover illustration: Patrick McEvoy
Editing by Ed Day
Interior art: Part pages © *Trees & Leaves,* Dover Publications, New York, 2004
    Article Illustrations © Chris Down (pages 26, 43, 53, 57, 80, 121,
        145, 152, 157, 185, 192)
     All other art © Clipart.com

Llewellyn Publications is a registered trademark of Llewellyn Worldwide Ltd.

Library of Congress Cataloging-in-Publication Data (Pending)
978-0-7387-3389-0

Llewellyn Publications does not participate in, endorse, or have any authority or responsibility concerning private business transactions between our authors and the public.

 Any Internet references contained in this work are current at publication time, but the publisher cannot guarantee that a specific location will continue to be maintained. Please refer to the publisher's website for links to authors' websites and other sources.

Llewellyn Publications
A Division of Llewellyn Worldwide Ltd.
2143 Wooddale Drive
Woodbury, MN 55125-2989
www.llewellyn.com

Printed in the United States of America

Contents

Foreword

Back in 1990, Llewellyn Publications decided to publish an annual Magical Almanac and I was asked to edit it. It promised to be a lot of fun, with the whole world of magic open to us. I hoped to get articles from the wide range of authors who produced books for the publisher. Alas, they were very slow in getting on board. The result was that I ended up writing much of the first issue myself! But slowly and surely the *Magical Almanac* gained ground and it wasn't long before I had a wide variety of articles from which to choose each year.

From the beginning, however, there was always one fellow author I could count on—Scott Cunningham. He and I lived not far from one another, in San Diego, and were good friends. We had similar interests and, as it happened, a similar sense of humor! I always knew that if I ran short of material, and the deadline was drawing near, I could give

Scott a call and he'd produce something for me. "Dressing With Power," "Magic in Hawaii," "Yule Lore," "The Magical Teacher," "Magic and Technology," "The Magical Pantry," "A Snow Spell," and "Spells" were all articles of Scott's that appeared in the first couple of editions.

The *Magical Almanac* grew in popularity over the years. I continued as editor for the first three years and then, in 1993, Scott joined me and we became co-editors. When introducing him to the readership at that time I stated, "He's happiest when reading or writing, but can be impossible to get off the phone!" I also noted that Scott had a collection of hermit crabs. For that edition Robin Wood also joined us as designer and her artistic sense made a big improvement to the almanac.

Scott wrote the introduction for that 1993 Almanac and in it he said, "The shadowy realm of magic has always had its share of adherents, in all ages. Unchained by rigidly mundane thought, magicians carve their futures with timeless spells, working with the powers of the Earth, Sun, Moon, the planets, and the elements to create positive change. Forging their lives with the forces of nature and their own energies, such magicians (power workers) discover that life is a series of opportunities undreamt of by most of their peers." Scott was himself most certainly one of those power workers.

–Raymond Buckland

Personal Power
and Growth

Dressing with Power

◇◇◇◇◇◇◇◇◇◇

*(Scott Cunningham defines magic as "the projection of
natural but subtle energies to produce needed change."
This article is the result of his ongoing investigation into
the ways that we can bring magic into our daily lives.)*

These days there's much talk about "power lunches," "power
cars," and "power colors" for clothes. The premise behind
this—the image you present will help you move up in the
world—has nothing to do with this article. Power, here, is
seen as the real thing—the juice that fuels magic. All things

that exist, including color, contain energy. Because clothing is colored, it can be used for magical purposes just as can crystals, herbs, music, food, and virtually anything else.

This is an age-old practice. An excellent example of the special uses of clothing today are the robes worn by some ritual magicians and Wiccans (Witches). These are usually hooded, made of natural fibers, and worn solely for ritual purposes. They may be embroidered with specific designs or left plain. Such robes are usually donned to awaken the "magical personality" of the practitioner in order to prepare his or her consciousness at every level for the rite to be performed.

That's all very well and good, but our everyday clothing presents us with powerful possibilities for improving our lives, for shaping our future into more positive experiences. Anyone can practice clothing magic and, indeed, the art of dressing can be a magical one.

First, the color of the clothes we wear—both those that can be seen by others as well as those that cannot—is of vital importance. Just as colors in our environment affect us, so too do the colors of our apparel. Some general ideas regarding the colors of clothing and their magical effects follow, but a few words are appropriate here:

- To bring a specific color's influence into your life, be aware of it. Look at your clothing during the day and feel its energy seeping inside you. Make dressing itself a ritual. As you slip on the first garment of the color you've chosen to help you, visualize that power becoming a part of you. Accept it.

- You needn't wear an entire outfit of a single color. As long as some of your clothing is of the needed color, it can work its magic. (If, for example, a man would feel uncomfortable wearing pink, simply wear it where it won't be seen—undershirts, socks, etc.)

- When you've accomplished your goal, move on to a new color and a new goal. Continuing to wear one color day after day may cause imbalances—three months of wearing nothing but blue may make you depressed; too much red can make steam boil out of your ears! Keep it in balance.

- Dirty clothing won't work properly. If you decide to use clothing as tools of magic, "ritually" prepare them by washing at frequent intervals.

- Remember to allow the color's energy to affect you. Invite it inside—don't just put on a red shirt and expect it to do all the work. Prepare yourself for the coming change.

- As will be seen in the following discussion, specific colors of clothing can be worn during specific magical acts to enhance their effectiveness.

The Colors

Wear **white** clothing for purification. This is excellent for ridding yourself of depression, for removing doubt, for freeing yourself from past negative habits. White clothing is, of course, also fine for use during all rituals of purification. It's a natural at the time of the full moon. Wear it to find peace within yourself.

Pink clothing promotes love. If you tend to go through your day (at work or at play) with an aggressive negative approach, pink clothing soothes you and produces a more pleasant personality. It is also ideal when relaxing with a loved one or when looking for an interpersonal relationship.

To attract attention and objects to yourself, **orange** is an excellent color. This color is a powerful drawing force. It is also fine to wear during solar rituals, for getting noticed in a crowd, and also when asking for promotions.

Red clothing produces physical energy. If you need to work long hours to accomplish something, or if you just can't seem to wake up in the morning, put on some red clothing and let its energy get you started and keep you going until the task is completed. At one time, red clothing was thought to protect children. Today we see it as a protective color because its energies are strong enough to deflect outside influences. This isn't an appropriate color for outgoing, aggressive people—they don't need red.

To improve your mind, wear **yellow** clothing. This color stimulates the conscious mind and may be of help while studying, memorizing, or trying to absorb new information. If you're forgetful, try putting on something yellow. Hats, of course, would be very appropriate.

Green clothing was once thought to be unlucky—especially for brides. In Ireland, the color itself was long considered to be taboo due to its connections with the fairies. Even green foods weren't eaten. However, green is an excellent color to wear to expand your ability to receive money, to promote spiritual as well as physical fertility, and, according to some traditions, maintaining good health.

Blue is considered to be a fortunate color for clothing nearly all around the world. One old rhyme says:

Always wear threads of blue,
Keep danger far from you.

It was once thought to protect its wearer from insults. From a magical perspective, blue clothing awakens psychic consciousness and so it is excellent for promoting intuition. It is worn when seeking psychic information. Blue is also a healing color suitable for resolving physical, mental, and emotional problems.

Violet or **lavender** clothing is ideal for slipping into meditative states—which isn't the best thing if you happen to be driving! At home, however, violet clothing (even just a T-shirt) can be worn for times of quiet contemplation or for spiritual activities.

When performing magical rituals, **purple** is the color of choice, for this hue is linked with akasha, the power of the universe. Its other association with riches may have something to do with a recent stint as the power color among men in the corporate world.

Brown clothing is suitable for peaceful moments. It blends into the Earth and is comforting and nourishing. Animals respond favorably to this color, but this won't necessarily halt attacks of vicious dogs.

Gray is a neutral color with little magical effect. It is suitable for general clothing.

Black clothing still frightens many. The heroes in old movies wore white while the "bad guys" wore black (symbolizing evil). However, black is no more evil than the night. For many, black clothing acts as a shield that guards the wearer from outside influences and energies. It is a color of protection. Wear it when you don't wish to be unduly noticed by others. Many ritualists wear black robes during magical workings because of its links with outer space and the deities who created all that exists.

The magical effects of **multicolored** clothing depend, of course, on the colors used in the material. Harsh slashes of bright red across cool blue may produce magical chaos for some while others will feel no ill effects at all. Still, this confusing pattern may be protective. Experiment with clothing of this kind (if you already have it) to find out how it affects you.

Plaids, the generic tartans that continue to be used in clothing for men and women, are longtime protective patterns. Those incorporating red into the design are excellent for this use. The intersecting lines bind and guard the wearer.

The Materials, and More

As to the type of materials: to put it bluntly, swear off polyester and other synthetic fabrics, at least for outerwear. I have no desire to walk around in a plastic bag, which is just what these things are. Synthetic materials are, after all, synthetic—and not useful in magic.

Cotton, linen, and wool, while being more expensive, are ideal materials for magic. In the past, wool was thought to lead to sexual desires and so its use was restricted from those on spiritual quests. This may also be the reason why linen became so popular among the Western clergy. All I've noticed from wool in general—setting color aside for a moment—is that it's scratchy. Cotton is the best material to use for virtually all your magical clothing.

If you have success with clothing magic, the horizons are unlimited. You may decide to dye your own clothing to produce the exact shade desired. Tie-dyeing produces a look that is once again popular, and these designs are protective. Those who embroider can sew symbols onto their clothing for specific purposes. Personal "luck" signs, runes, and planetary symbols are all appropriate.

Virtually every article of clothing, from shoes and socks to scarves and hats, is infused with ancient magic. For example, did you know that high-heeled shoes are thought to be protective? (They may be, but they kill the feet!) Those waiting for a complicated matter to be brought to a conclusion were once directed to blow up a sleeve. And did you ever wonder why some dark-colored socks have white toes? They were originally made this way to protect the wearer from being tripped by elves.

Superstitions regarding clothes abound. Don't put hats and shoes on the bed. Tie knots in a piece of your mate's underwear to ensure fidelity. If you accidentally put on an article of clothing inside-out, you should wear it that way for good luck. Or, if you're having a bad day, take off your clothing and put it on inside-out to bring positive changes. Such popular beliefs are half-remembered survivals of rituals performed long ago. They point to the power that earlier humans saw in clothing.

Granted, this magic isn't for those who follow the dictates of high fashion, who allow others to say what's "in" and what to wear. It is for true individualists who are looking to take control of their clothing and their lives.

So the next time you look at your wardrobe and sigh to yourself "What should I wear today?" think about this article—and dress with power!

Magical Secrecy

◇◇◇◇◇◇◇◇◇◇

One of the basic principles of magic, as we are often taught, is *secrecy*. Don't speak of your magical workings, we're told. Don't tell your friends of your interest in magic, let alone discuss the candle ritual that you performed last night.

Be still, we're taught. Talk not. Let the power cook. Some say that by speaking of your magical operations, you'll disperse the energies that you've put into them. Others state that nonmagicians, upon hearing of a magical ritual that you've performed, will send out unbelieving, negative energies that will block your spell from manifesting. A few magicians will say that secrecy about one's magical proclivities was once a necessity for saving one's neck. Others give no reason. They simply repeat the old code: "Be silent."

Is this superstition? Perhaps. Many magicians, who work with energies that scientists haven't yet been able to locate or identify, simply don't know everything about these energies. They may have seen the effectiveness of rituals that they've performed. They may even have told close friends about these rituals prior to their manifestations, with no ill effects. But soon, the secrecy issue begins ringing a bell.

"Should I talk about these things?" they'll ask themselves. "After all, that book stated that loose lips sink spells. That woman I know does rituals all the time, but only tells me about them *after* they've taken effect. And I'm sure that there are lots of magicians who'd never breathe a word about that blue candle that they've been burning, their herbal baths, their visualizations, or chants or moonlit rites."

Doubt soon clouds the magician's mind. Eventually, the magician buttons up and doesn't speak of rituals. Secrecy has once again been conferred on the process.

This is unfortunate and unnecessary. True magic, the movement of natural energies to create needed change, is limitless. Speaking of a ritual to others doesn't disperse the energies. On the contrary, it gives you a new opportunity to send more power toward your magical goal.

Disbelief also isn't a satisfactory reason for magical secrecy. The disbelief of others has about as much effect on magic as does an unschooled person's doubt that a calculator can add

2 and 2 to equal 4. The calculator will work regardless of this observer's doubt. So, too, will magic.

There are other reasons why the calculator possibly wouldn't perform this simple operation: faulty microchips, low battery power, a lack of batteries, an operator who pushes the wrong buttons, or a switch turned to "off." But an observer's disbelief can't be the cause.

The same is true of magic. Properly performed, magic will be effective. If energy is raised within the body, programmed with intent, and projected toward its goal with the proper force and visualization, it will be effective. Perhaps not overnight. Many repetitions of the magical ritual may be necessary. But it usually is effective if the operator (the magician) knows how to use this process.

The problem of magical secrecy is the doubt that it instills within the magician. If a magician believes that speaking of her or his rituals to others will somehow diminish their power, it just might—precisely because of this belief. This is similar to going to bed late one night, all the time thinking, "I just know I'll sleep in tomorrow morning and be late for work," and doing just that. This is negative programming, and negative programming is remarkably effective.

The third reason often proffered for magical secrecy, that it's a tradition handed down from earlier times when magicians were rounded up and charged with heresy, is at least historically accurate. But speaking of rituals to close friends today isn't likely to cause you to be hanged.

Secrecy, then, isn't a necessary part of magic. It's no guarantee of magical success. This doesn't mean that you should walk around wearing a green button that states, "I did a money ritual last night!" It also doesn't mean that you *must* discuss your magical affairs with others, especially if you're working on intensely private matters.

You certainly may wish to be silent about your magical rituals among friends who know of your interests, and even among other magicians. If so, be certain of the reasons you're silent.

Magical secrecy concerning rituals is a superstition that should have no place in our lives.

The Sorceress:
A Fable by Aesop

◇◇◇◇◇◇◇◇◇◇

*Night had stilled the whole world, silencing the
tongues of every creature. Trees swayed as they drowsed
above sleeping bushes. The forest was hushed.*

*A sorceress, a rare woman versed in the arts of fearful
magic, entered the gloomy forest. She made a large circle,
set up a tripod, and burned fragrant vervain as she
intoned ancient incantations.*

*Her dreadful words resounded through the air, awakening
every creature, plant, and tree for miles around.*

The sorceress blew her mystic words on the wind,
disturbing cattle and people in far distant places.
The countryside shivered.

Her impassioned incantation even drew the loon itself
into the wood to assist in her magical quest. In the eerie
light, spirits of the long dead appeared before the sorceress
in shadowy forms, demanding to know why they had been
awakened from their long sleep.

"Tell me," she said, her face lightened by the triangular
flames of the smoldering vervain. "Tell me where
I can find what I have lost: my favorite little dog!"

"Impudent creature!" the spirits shouted in unison.
"Must the order of nature be reversed and the sleep of
every creature be disturbed for the sake of your little dog?"

Moral: Don't waste great powers on trivial matters!

The Lore of Money

◇◇◇◇◇◇◇◇◇◇

Money is a relatively new idea. In the past, when civilization had just been born, goods and services were usually bartered: "Two bushels of apples for ten quarts of milk." Money was invented as a perfect means of exchange. It was compact (far easier to move about than a cow) and could be used to purchase nearly anything—so long as the seller recognized the buyer's currency. Money soon became an established part of human existence. It also garnered its share of lore and magic. Here are some delightful "old wisdoms," lore and spells concerning cash:

- Always keep at least a few coins in your home when leaving it for a journey or vacation. To do otherwise bodes ill.

- If you drop any money while in the home, say "Money on the floor, money at the door." Step on the money and pick it up; more will come to you.

- Finding money is quite fortunate, but to keep such money is thought to invite misfortune. Spend it as quickly as possible, and tell no one of its origin.

- Never leave the house without at least one coin in your pocket or handbag. The best charm of all is a bent coin or a coin pierced with a hole. Carrying one of these is both "lucky" and quite protective.

- If you must fold your bills, fold them toward you, for this indicates that money will come to you. Folding money away from you will result in its quick absence.

- Finding a coin minted in the year of your birth is an exceptionally fortunate blessing. This is the one type of "found money" that should be retained. Safeguard it as a charm and never spend it.

- Before midnight on New Year's Eve, place a small amount of silver money somewhere outside. Retrieve it the next morning on New Year's Day and your earnings during the next year will be greater than your bills.

- On New Year's Day, rub yourself with a silver coin for money all year.

- To ensure that you will always have money and friends, tie a string into a circle and keep it in your pocket, wallet, or purse.

- While becalmed at sea, throw a coin into the water; the winds will immediately fill the sails. (In England, a sixpence was always used.)

- Hold a silver coin in your hand, look over your shoulder at the first star that appears at dusk, and make a wish.

- Turn silver money on the night of the New Moon to secure prosperity.

- Dreaming of money for three nights in a row indicates that money will soon come to the dreamer.

- Counting your money too often means that it will soon be gone.

- Rub a small green candle with powdered cloves. Place it and its holder on top of a new dollar bill. Three hours after sunset on a Thursday evening, light the candle and let it burn until it has gone out the next day, bury the candle stub; rub the dollar bill with powdered cloves and hide it in the house.

Protective Magics

◇◇◇◇◇◇◇◇◇◇

Though we live in a highly civilized society, there are times when it is wise to guard ourselves: hearing a sound in the house at night, walking a lonely stretch of road, driving on a busy highway. At such moments, simple, quick, protective rites can put our minds at ease and strengthen our psychic armor. Here are some of my favorites:

In Bed

When lying in bed at night, visualize yourself completely encased in a glowing purple suit of power through which no energy can pass.

When Driving at Night

Visualize a huge pentagram (five-pointed star) out of brilliant white light. "Wrap" this around your car. Say any short, quick protective chant such as the following:

Bound, bound, bound,
Wound around;
Guard me now,
Sky to ground.

(This chant can be used with other forms of protection.)

Outside at Night

Straighten your back. Breathe slowly. Visualize yourself as a lion stalking the jungle, searching for prey. Transmit the unmistakable image that you're not to be bothered by anyone.

When Someone
Tries to Read Your Thoughts

If you believe that someone is trying to read your thoughts or otherwise intrude into your head, visualize it as being stuffed with thick mashed potatoes that make such penetration impossible.

Children

As children leave the house, throw a bit of sand, salt, birdseed, or sugar after them while saying:

Danger begone;
Be dispersed!
I now bind
Up the curse!

For Many Circumstances

- Taste salt, or throw it around you in a circle (carrying a small packet of salt from a restaurant facilitates this).

- Create a glowing sphere of energy around your body with your mind. Strengthen it and know that it's truly there. Charge it to guard and protect you.

- Cross your fingers (this spell calls upon the sun).

- Tighten your muscles and relax them while visualizing protection. (This sends out protective power.)

- Look at something white (and call its protective energies to you).

- Stand. (You're more in control when standing than when sitting or reclining.)

Though you'll have few opportunities to use such information, it's a wise magician who has at least one of these techniques memorized and ready for immediate use—just in case the need arises.

Magical Names

◇◇◇◇◇◇◇◇◇◇

Upon initiation into a mystic group, or even when seriously taking up their studies and practices, many magicians adopt a magical name. This long-standing tradition is based upon the concept that the new name:

- Symbolizes the person's new magical personality

- Celebrates her or his entrance into the art or group

- Subtly changes the person, shifting her or his consciousness to a more magical alignment

There are many methods of choosing such names, and the options are quite broad. Names of famous persons, deities, and creatures from world mythology can be chosen, as can those of animals, plants, and flowers.

Some magicians rely on numerology or divination to find the most suitable name.

Once adopted, the magical name becomes a powerful and direct connection with the person's magical practices. Thus, it is rarely revealed to nonpractitioners. (A "public" magical name can also be adopted and shared.)

In choosing a name, much research is often necessary to be certain that the name is consistent with the personality of the person who is to use it. This is of vital importance when using names drawn from history or ancient religions.

The following list includes some common magical names, past and present. (Though divided here by sex, a few of these can be used by either women or men.)

Women

Albina	Elspeth	Pye
Almathea	Flora	Rhea
Ariadne	Grammercie	Rhiannon
Aster	Heather	Selene
Branwen	Isobel	Senara
Bridget	Lucina	Taweret
Covantina	Marian	Theos
Dana	Morgana	Vivienne
Diana	Nimue	

Men

Andras	Emrys	Puck
Andro	Gwdion	Robin
Arthur	Gwyn	Skylld
Artisson	Helios	Sylvanus
Belinus	Janara	Taliesin
Bran	Llyr	Tyr
Cyprian	Mansurin	Verdelet
Dalan	Math	Wayland
Dylan	Myrrdyn	Wepwawet

Tattooing

◇◇◇◇◇◇◇◇◇◇

The technique of creating permanent pictures on the human body by inserting dyes under the skin has been in use for well over 4,000 years. Even some Egyptian mummies show some traces of the process.

The word "tattoo" stems from the Tahitian *tatua*, and was introduced to Europe by Captain Cook after his visit to Tahiti in 1769. Tattooing is a complex subject, owing to its world-wide distribution and the great variety of cultural reasons for its usage.

Tattooing was practiced in ancient times in North America, Peru, Mexico, Britain, Greece, Australia, New Zealand, Greenland, India, China, Japan, Tahiti, Easter Island, Hawaii, and throughout the South Pacific.

In some places, it served as a sign of social caste, as in Hawaii, where slaves were tattooed on their faces. In other places and times, it was a requirement of initiation into a religion (as an ordeal), a form of medicine, or a practice directly linked with magic.

Recently, persons have been tattooed to graphically demonstrate contempt (i.e., images of wartime enemies) or membership in secret (and unlawful) societies such as the Yakuza in Japan and American street and prison gangs. Tattooing is also seen today as a form of self-expression unrelated to any other concerns.

Tattoos, however, have also been magical. They can be considered to be permanent amulets (objects designed to avert evil) or talismans (to attract positive influences) that their bearers are incapable of losing.

Aboriginal Australians had their upper arms tattooed to repel boomerangs (used as weapons). Women in Burma had a triangular tattoo applied to their lips or tongues to attract love, and Ainu women of old Japan tattooed themselves during epidemics as a protectant against disease.

Some Middle Eastern women were tattooed with dots around the navel on the second or third day of menstruation to ensure pregnancy. Eagles are tattooed onto Middle Eastern men to ensure strength.

Tattooing has also had religious associations. Plateau Indians of North America were tattooed on their faces and bodies with the symbols of their guardian spirits. The eunuch priests of Attis in ancient Phrygia were tattooed with ivy-leaf patterns. In certain parts of India, those that died untattooed weren't ushered into the underworld after death.

Tattoos were also considered to be efficacious remedies. In Bengal, tattoos cured goiters. The Andawanese used tattoos to relieve headache, toothache, and rheumatism. Some people in Japan had themselves tattooed to reverse failing eyesight; in Egypt, tattoos of small birds near the eyes were considered effective for this purpose until quite recently.

Throughout the Middle East, men and women are tattooed with as simple a design as a single black dot near an injury (such as a sprain) to speed its healing.

During this century, few sailors didn't sport at least one tattoo. Specific designs (horseshoes, black cats, and four-leaf clovers) were considered effective charms against drowning (the ever-present threat to those on the sea), and a tattoo of any design was sadly thought to prevent its bearer from contracting sexually transmitted diseases.

In the Western world, tattooing has undergone periods of tolerance and intolerance. Some clergymen preached that the Bible forbade it, but many who were tattooed (including members of British royalty) simply didn't care.

To this day, tattooing is an exotic art, considered by the unpatterned majority to be of interest only to those on the fringes of society: sailors, prostitutes, musicians, motorcycle riders, gang members, and thieves. Tattooing's well-known associations with pre-Christian religion and magic are partially responsible for this, as is the well-known Biblical passage prohibiting its use (Lev. 19:28).

Still, for many, adopting a tattoo is a semispiritual experience, which begins with the first urges, continues through selection (or creation) of the design, and culminates in the actual process. Manly contemporary persons choose to tattoo themselves to signify their power over their bodies and souls, as manifestations of their achievement of higher spiritual awareness.

The discomfort involved in receiving the tattoo, they state, is an important and necessary part of what many perceive to be an initiatory process. On one Pacific island, a chant runs:

Short is the pain, long the decoration.
Short, short is the pain, long the decoration.

Tattoos, then, are many things to many persons. In their earliest forms, however, they were magical amulets and talismans that assisted the living and ensured their place in the underworld when this life was over.

Magical Household Hints

◇◇◇◇◇◇◇◇◇◇

- Freeze candles before use to make them last longer.

- Keep an onion in the kitchen to guard against magical contamination.

- When cleaning your home, begin in the east-facing room(s) and continue clockwise until the house is finished.

- To quickly polish silver jewelry or silver magical tools before ritual, wet and lightly rub with baking soda. This is for emergencies only; repeated application will pit the silver.

- Burn frankincense or sandalwood once a month to magically freshen your home.

- Make a small "ritual kit" out of a box or basket. Into this put a small knife, a stick (wand), a small cup, and a flat stone. Add also a small white candle and holder, a small bottle of pure water, matches, an incense stick or cone and tiny packages of rose petals, rosemary, and salt. With this ritual kit you can perform rites of all types at a moment's notice, without having to collect the objects to be used. This is quite useful for emergencies.

- Pour a bit of vinegar down each drain monthly on the night before the New Moon to purify your home.

- Add a few drops of the pure essential oil of lavender or hyssop to wash water when cleaning ritual garments (such as robes). This magically cleanses them.

- Burn citronella candles during outdoor rituals at night to guard against flying insects.

- Always eat after magical rites. A glass of milk, a piece of bread, an apple—ingest food to return your consciousness to this world.

- Muffle smoke detectors (or move far away from them) when performing magical rituals indoors that involve many candles or much incense.

- To remove dried candle wax from altar cloths, robes, and even carpets, place the soiled cloth on a flat surface. Lay a piece of cotton cloth on top of this. Iron with a warm iron and the cotton will absorb the wax. (Warning: red candle wax creates indelible stains. The wax can be removed, but not the red stain.)

- Save leftover candle stubs in separate containers (by color). When you have a large collection of one hue, melt them in a double boiler, and dip lengths of wicking into the wax to create new candles.

- Burns from candles, incense, charcoal, matches, heated censers, and cauldrons can be quickly quenched by application of the gel from the aloe vera plant.

- To freshen the air without the use of synthetic sprays before ritual, hang bunches of fresh mint, dill, and other aromatic plants near the ceiling.

- Keep your musical notebooks and secret texts in a locked cabinet. If this isn't possible, protect these texts from the eyes of others by placing a small bottle filled with pins and salt on the shelf behind the spellbooks.

Once a spell has been completed, never let the tools used for it sit idle. Put the objects away when the spell is over.

Magic and Technology

◇◇◇◇◇◇◇◇◇◇

The magician eases into a tub of scented water. She closes her eyes and relaxes to the sound of flutes playing on her tape recorder. Shadows dance across her eyelids from a nearby candle flame.

After a few minutes, she rises, dries her body, slips into a white cotton robe, places a shimmering pentagram around her neck, and walks into her bedroom.

From the compartment beneath a flat wooden table she removes a small knife, a silver cup, a bottle of salt, an incense burner, piles of crystals, and bottles of herbs: the tools of magic.

Moments later, she strikes a match and begins her ritual of natural magic, causing the energies within herself to echo those in the stones and herbs which she's piled onto her altar, unaware that every object she has touched has also been touched by technology.

———

I resisted bringing a computer into my life for many years. I thought that my magical writings would suffer by using such a technologically advanced instrument. Distancing myself even further from the sharpened pen and inkwell meant that my writings would lose their magic. Or so I thought.

Circumstances changed all that. My father gave me his old computer. It took me a few days to learn how to use it. I bore on, and soon I was writing like never before. No typewriter that I had ever used could keep up with the rough copy that spilled from me. My little Radio Shack TRS-80 almost kept up, and I soon changed my mind.

Like many natural magicians, I have often deplored the misuse of technology in our world. Not the technology itself, but its nonevolutionary applications. As a child, growing up and struggling to understand the mechanisms of nature and of magic, I also had to become familiar with the newer mechanisms that our species was producing. As I studied and learned, I knew with all the wisdom of a fifteen-year-old that magic and technology would never merge.

How times change. Once I began actually writing on a computer (and I've now done at least fifteen books on this contraption), I realized that a typewriter is also a product of technology as is the earlier moveable type, the fountain pen, the pencil, and a sharpened stick deliberately burned to produce a charcoaled writing tip. Any object altered or deliberately made by a human being, from a candle to a space shuttle, represents applied technology.

I was forced to reassess my views. Technology, in itself, isn't bad. It certainly supplies many of the tools of magic (censers, swords and knifes, robes, jewelry, cups, and cauldrons). It is also used to process other tools (cutting herbs, shaping or polishing stones, fashioning wands). Such innovations as optical scanners, computerized typesetting, and high-speed printing have allowed millions of hungry readers to explore various methods of folk magic.

The mythical magician that we met in the beginning of this article was blissfully ignorant that technology serves all aspects of human life, not just the materially based avenues. The very tools that she used were crafted—manufactured.

A fiftyish, bearded man who leaves his commodities brokerage to live in a lamasery in Tibet has to rely on technology (in this case, a high-speed jet) to get to his spiritual retreat. The survivalist who flakes obsidian to make a knife has also used technology.

As we leave the 1980s behind us, many magicians are reaping the benefits that technology has to offer. Personal spell books, once copied by hand in candlelit rooms, are now being keyed onto floppy discs. Rituals printed in dot matrix are handed out to members of magical groups. Magical computer bulletin boards are flourishing, and many a magician amasses large phone bills by off-loading spells and rituals from peers thousands of miles away.

But as we fully embrace technology, as we enjoy the unquestionable benefits that it has given us, it is vitally important to remember our Earth roots. Technology can be so dazzling that we can forget to look beyond it.

———

Play your compact discs during ritual. Computerize your rituals and spells. Use polished stones and artificially dried herbs. But keep firmly in mind what we're supposed to be doing: merging our energies with those of the Earth and Her treasures to improve our lives.

Even a polyester cord or floppy disc started out as a subterranean pool of crude oil. Your cotton robe once nodded in warm breezes in the American South, in Egypt, or some other place on the globe. The paper upon which these words are printed is a byproduct (a "waste") of the lumber industry. Think of the origins of your magical tools before you use them. Find their Earth energies still pulsing within them.

Magic, as a tool of self-transformation, can never be divorced from technology. It is our responsibility to ensure that our magic is never divorced from the Earth.

The practice of magic is a use of applied technology. Use it wisely.

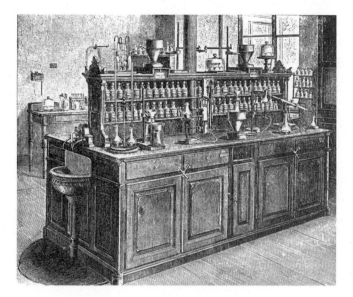

Science and Magic

◇◇◇◇◇◇◇◇◇◇

Magic is the utilization of natural energies to cause positive transformations. Science constitutes careful inquiry into nature, its principles, and manifestations. When we speak of "science," we're referring to that body of knowledge that has been ascertained through observation, investigation, critical analysis, and systemization and that has been lumped together into convenient principles. Science is allegedly "exact," without room for error.

For over 400 years, "science" has claimed that magic isn't effective, since it cannot be studied through conventional methods, and its practitioners aren't operating with any known natural laws.

This doesn't bother magicians, who continue to use their art to better their lives. But even scientists admit that they don't know everything about our world. If they did, the field of scientific inquiry would no longer exist.

Many scientists, however, fail to recognize that their vision of natural law is far too narrow to provide a complete picture. They've discovered and evaluated A, B, C, D, and E, and fail to look any further. Meanwhile, magicians are actively using F, G, H, I, J, K, L, and M.

Much of what was once considered to be supernatural has now been investigated and added to the body of scientifically "proven" lore, such as magnetism, psychology, medicine, mathematics, positive thinking, and so on. Yet science has largely been unable to move further, to step away from comfortable concepts and enter the realm of nonphysical energies and their effects.

In the end, though, this will occur. Science always vindicates magic. It is up to science to explain magic and the practice's underlying principles.

Though tunnel vision and a total lack of interdisciplinary information exchange is hampering most scientists in their quest for knowledge, many physicists are currently producing and testing theories that knock on magic's inner door. In time, they may be able to explain, at least theoretically, some of the "whys" of magic.

Until that day, however, magicians will continue to practice their ancient art, secure in the knowledge that it is effective, and rightfully ignoring the "scientific" howls of protest.

Many magicians have investigated magic to the extent of their abilities. They've also observed its effects, and have built up a body of knowledge concerning its practice. Experiments (spells) have been successfully replicated time and time again. This is one of the keys to admission into scientific knowledge; the successful replication of experiments or trials that prove underlying theories, no matter how unusual they may seem.

However, magic is far more ethereal than is cell division, magnetism, or photosynthesis. Much of it occurs within the magician and thus cannot be adequately recorded. Devices with the sensitivity to measure the energies at work in magic have not yet been created, and the effects of successful magic can be ascribed to a number of other causes.

And so magic cannot yet be "scientifically" proved. However, the fault lies not in the practice, but in archaic technology and the unwillingness of the scientific community to look beyond its limited view and to gaze at the dazzling *true* world just beyond its comprehension.

Instruction and Applied Magic

The Magical Teacher

◇◇◇◇◇◇◇◇◇◇

Originally, she lived in the last house on the outskirts of the village. Or he may have dwelled on a mountaintop. She could have been a wandering mystic; he, a hermit, enclosed in a turret with a view of miles of countryside.

These were special persons, living outside the boundaries of society, possessed of the "mystic temperament." (Thanks to Ray T. Malbrough, author of *Charms, Spells & Formulas*, for this term) that impelled them to seek out lonely places. In their isolation they studied plants, minerals, the stars, and arcane manuscripts. Every morning, villagers and farmers would come to their homes, bearing vegetables and chickens, along with requests for ritual acts. By moonlight, the magicians would work the rituals that brought the people's needs into manifestation.

After many years of such an existence, a student appeared, moved in, and began learning the ancient secrets. The magician became the magical teacher. Watching and listening, the student eventually reaped the benefits of a lifetime of lonely practice.

This romantic vision of past magicians, and of the manner in which they trained their successors, lives on in the dreams of contemporary practitioners. Oh, to go back to those times and learn from a real teacher! To live a fully magical life unhindered by a job, bills, taxes, and other unnecessary distractions of our everyday lives!

The vision is appealing, but it is no longer possible. We exist in a highly technological world. The most remote places can be reached in a few days by jet, automobile, train, horseback, and/or on foot. The old ways—the old magicians—are still present in what we ungraciously term "Third World countries," but they are apt to listen to the radio at night, vote, and register their cars. Spells may be interrupted by the ringing of telephones, and hard currency often replaces the food once used as payment for their ritual works.

Yet, the dream continues. People still feel that they need teachers, those gifted individuals who can distill the fruits of their experiences and pass them on to others. Seekers read books and magazines, attend classes and workshops. If they're willing to part with a great deal of money, they spend a weekend with a highly visible expert to learn of shamanism, healing, crystals, and many other topics—in the company of 100 to 300 other fellow seekers.

After the flurry of learning, after the chants have been memorized and the notes filed away, even after the student has become proficient at magic, she or he may yearn for more: a wandering mystic with all knowledge. A hermit. Moonlit rituals at the side of an untamed magician locked in the fastness of a primeval forest!

Such things were possible only during earlier times, when few cared to penetrate the artificial veil that societies create between the physical and the nonphysical worlds. There were few teachers, but that didn't matter because there were few students. Today, when tens of thousands desire to penetrate that veil to learn of magic, there aren't enough teachers to fulfill their needs. A direct, face-to-face, one-on-one learning experience simply isn't possible for all seekers.

What's the answer for the many thousands of disappointed seekers?

Study what you would, and learn your subject well. Comb new and used bookstores for works that cover your area of interest. Frequent your local library. Read everything, but read with discrimination. Remember, not all books are reliable.

Apply this learning by performing rituals. By actually doing this, you'll learn from your mistakes. These lessons can be more valuable than those you'd otherwise receive from a teacher.

Keep records. If you aren't a diligent journaler, at least jot down important facts that you've learned in your practice.

Go to the source. Once a week, once a month, or once a year, leave civilization behind and commune with nature. Spend an hour or a weekend in a cave, on a mountain, in the desert. Sense the overwhelming energy of the Earth and your own connection with it inside yourself. Know that as a magician it is these energies that you utilize to create positive change. It is wise to recharge your psychic batteries at regular intervals.

Finally, *listen to nature.* Nature is the original teacher—She who taught the first magicians. Study the movement of leaves and the ways of animals. Listen to the wind, to the rush of water, to millions of grains of sand bouncing against each other. Watch the sunrise and the sunset. Feel the cycles of the Earth pulsing within yourself.

Nature is the great Mistress of Secrets. If you would be taught, allow yourself to learn. The lessons are all around us in the natural world. We simply have to recapture the ability to hear and to see them.

Continue your search for a teacher, if you feel that it is necessary. You may well find one, but continue to teach yourself.

Study, apply your learning, keep records, go to the source and listen to nature. If you're serious about making magic a part of your life, you'll eventually realize that you've found the teacher you've always wanted.

And it will be you.

Magical Words:
A Short Glossary

◇◇◇◇◇◇◇◇◇◇

Amulet: A magically empowered object that deflects specific (usually negative) energies. It may be carried, worn, or put in a specific place. Compare with **Talisman**.

Bane: That which destroys life; is useless, poisonous, destructive, or evil.

Baneful: See **Bane**.

BCE: Before Common Era; the nonreligious equivalent of BC.

Beltane: A Wiccan religious festival, observed on April 30, that celebrates the burgeoning fertility of the Earth (and, for some Wiccans, the wedding of the Goddess and God).

Blessing: The act of conferring positive energy upon a person, place, or thing. It is usually a spiritual or religious practice.

CE: Common Era; the nonreligious equivalent of AD.

Charging: See **Empowering.**

Charm: A magically empowered object carried to attract positive energies.

Clockwise: The traditional form of movement in positive magic. (If you're standing facing a tree, move to your left and walk in a circle around it. That's clockwise motion.) Also known as deosil movement.

Conscious Mind: The analytical, materially based, rational half of our consciousness. Compare with **Psychic Mind.**

Coven: A closely-knit group of Wiccans who gather for religious observances and magic.

Cursing: The deliberate (and rare) movement of negative energies to affect a person, place, or thing.

Deosil: See **Clockwise.**

Divination: The magical art of discovering the unknown by interpreting random patterns or symbols. Sometimes incorrectly referred to as "fortune-telling."

Elements, The: Earth, Air, Fire, and Water. These four essences are the building blocks of the universe, and ancient magical sources of energy.

Empowering: The act of moving energy into an object.

Energy: A general term for the currently immeasurable (but real) power that exists within all natural objects and beings—including our own bodies. It is used in **Folk Magic.** See also **Personal Power.**

Folk Magic: The practice of magic utilizing **Personal Power,** in conjunction with natural tools, in a nonreligious framework, to cause positive change.

Herb: Virtually any plant used in magic.

Imbolc: A **Wiccan** religious festival celebrated on February 1st or 2nd that celebrates the first stirrings of spring.

Luck, Good: An individual's ability to make timely, correct decisions, to perform correct actions, and to place herself or himself in positive situations. "Bad luck" stems from ignorance and an unwillingness to accept self-responsibility.

Lughnasadh: A **Wiccan** religious festival celebrated on August 1st that marks the first harvest.

Magic: The movement of natural (yet subtle) **Energies** to manifest positive, needed change. Magic is the process of "rousing" energy, giving it purpose (through **Visualization**), and releasing it to create a change. This is a natural (not supernatural) practice.

Meditation: Reflection, contemplation, turning inward toward the self or outward toward Deity or nature.

Midsummer: The Summer Solstice, a **Wiccan** religious festival and a traditional time for magic.

Pagan: From the Latin **Paganus**, a "country dweller" or "villager." Today it's used as a general term for followers of **Wicca** and other polytheistic, magic-embracing religions. Pagans aren't Satanists, dangerous, or evil.

Pentagram: An interlaced five-pointed star (one point at its top) that has been used for thousands of years as a protective device. Today the pentagram is also associated with the **Element** of Earth and with **Wicca.** It has no evil associations.

Personal Power: That energy which sustains our bodies. We first absorb it from our biological mothers within the womb and, later, from food, water, the Moon and Sun, and other natural objects. We release personal power during stress, exercise, sex, conception, and childbirth. **Magic** is usually a movement of personal power for a specific goal.

Power: See **Energy; Personal Power.**

Psychic Attack: See **Cursing.**

Psychic Awareness: The act of being consciously psychic, in which the **Psychic Mind** and the **Conscious Mind** are linked and working in harmony.

Psychic Mind: The subconscious or unconscious mind, in which we receive psychic impulses. The psychic mind is at work when we sleep, dream, and meditate.

Rite: See **Ritual.**

Ritual: Ceremony. A specific form of movement, manipulation of objects, or inner processes designed to produce desired effects. In **Magic** it allows the magician to move energy toward needed goals. A **Spell** is a magical rite.

Runes: Stick-like figures, some of which are remnants of old Teutonic alphabets; others are pictographs. These symbols are once again being widely used in all forms of **Magic.**

Sabbat: A **Wiccan** religious festival.

Samhain: A **Wiccan** religious festival celebrated on October 31, which marks the last harvest and the preparations for winter.

Spell: The mainstay of **Folk Magic,** spells are simply magical rites. They're usually nonreligious and often include spoken words.

Spellcraft: An alternate term for **Folk Magic.**

Talisman: An object ritually **Charged** with power to attract a specific force or energy to its bearer. Compare with **Amulet.**

Visualization: The process of forming mental images. Magical visualization consists of forming images of needed goals during magic. It is a function of the **Conscious Mind.**

Widdershins: Counterclockwise ritual motion.

Wicca: A contemporary **Pagan** religion with spiritual roots in the earliest expressions of reverence of nature as a manifestation of the divine. Wicca views Deity as Goddess and God; thus it is polytheistic. It also embraces the practice of **Magic** and accepts reincarnation. Religious festivals are held in observance of the Full Moon and other astronomical (and agricultural) phenomena. It has no associations with Satanism.

Wiccan: Of or relating to **Wicca.**

Witch: Anciently, a European practitioner of pre-Christian **Folk Magic,** particularly that relating to herbs, healing, wells, rivers, and stones. One who practiced **Witchcraft.** Later, this term's meaning was deliberately altered to denote demented, dangerous beings who practiced destructive magic and who threatened Christianity. This latter definition is false. (Some Wiccans also use the word to describe themselves.)

Witchcraft: The craft of the Witch. Magic, especially magic utilizing **Personal Power** in conjunction with the energies within stones, herbs, colors, and other natural objects. While this does have spiritual overtones, witchcraft, according to this definition, isn't a religion. However, some followers of **Wicca** use this word to denote their religion.

Yule: A **Wiccan** religious festival celebrated on the Winter Solstice that marks the rebirth of the Sun.

Magical Rites

◇◇◇◇◇◇◇◇◇◇

Magic is an old friend. It's been part of the human experience since the earliest times. Wherever our ancestors wandered in antiquity, they brought with them their most important tools: fire-making stones, weapons, tools of cultivation, bone needles … and magic.

Many today see magic as fantasy: an impossible process recorded only in dusty fairy tales. Just as those who have never used flint might mistrust its use. In creating fire, so too has magic been viewed as a supernatural activity with no roots in reality.

All such doubts vanish in those who have experienced magic, for magic is an experiential art. Those who practice it no longer doubt its effectiveness precisely because they've reaped the benefits of this ancient form of transformation. Disbelief becomes knowledge. Only those who have never practiced magic can doubt it as a viable process.

Some claim that magic is supernatural, that its true power stems from evil. From this viewpoint, such persons should also view childbirth, germination of seeds, positive thinking (hope), love, spiritual awareness, exercise, the passage of the seasons, and all other aspects of life as supernatural, for the powers at work in these phenomena are identical with those used in magic.

This concept is, of course, born in those who are out of touch with the Earth and Her mysteries. In a day of artificiality, when we surround ourselves with the things of humans, touching nature can seem to be a dangerous and evil practice.

However, *magic* is a natural practice, and many of us find the time to explore its shaded byways, uncovering old spells and collecting magical regalia. Once we've discovered the information and have acquired the tools, we're equipped to utilize magic's timeless mysteries to improve our lives.

Though there are many theories regarding magic, there are some threads of thought that are common to most. These are:

- Magic is effective because it's natural.

- Magic utilizes natural (but subtle) energies.

- These energies stem from the practitioner, from nature and from certain objects (including candles, colors, stones, herbs, and symbols).

- The magician gathers these energies and transforms them within the self through visualization (the process of creating mental images of the needed change).

- The magician then directs these energies (into a stone, a charm, a river, a candle, an herb, the wind, the ocean, a mountain or cave, an animal or, in healing, a person) so that they can manifest. The magician may also redirect such energies back within herself or himself to create a more immediate personal change.

- Except in extraordinary situations, the changes created by magic won't instantaneously manifest. A day, week, or month (depending on the nature of the rite) may need to pass for the spell to come to fruition.

This guide to the rationale of magic is indeed simple, but is largely accepted by most magicians who've given thought to the inner workings of magic.

Magicians have centuries of guidelines to keep in mind while performing their rites. Despite popular misconceptions, magicians are often of the highest moral caliber. Some magician's rules include the following:

- Magic is used in emergencies or as the last resort. It isn't a shortcut.

- Magic is never used to manipulate (even in "positive" ways) another human being without her or his permission.

- Magic is never used to harm anyone or anything, anywhere, at any time, for any reason.

- The magician will not accept payment for magical workings (unless she or he lives in a cashless society, when food may be accepted in trade).

- Magic is a tool for love.

Such guidelines reveal that magic is far from an evil, antisocial art. On the contrary, magicians are utilizing power that has its ultimate source in the life force of the universe. To abuse this energy for destructive acts is against all magical principles. Magicians are the caretakers of the Earth and of all Her species.

The way of magic is the road less traveled. Many fear the responsibility that arcane wisdom brings. Others fear the night. But those of us who have walked this road and have discovered its wonders know that there is nothing to fear. Indeed, the path shines in full moonlight, and that which lies along its twisted way is friendly, comforting, and useful.

Magic may never again enjoy its former popularity, for time has greatly altered the world and all within it. Those of us who continue the old traditions do so out of love and hope. *We* light candles and smolder incense and pronounce mystic words by the crossroads, secure in our knowledge, and preparing for a brighter tomorrow.

Remedies of the Wise Women

◇◇◇◇◇◇◇◇◇◇

In rural areas today, and everywhere in the past, home remedies were used to treat a variety of illnesses and conditions. Though each family knew some cures or treatments, many villages had at least one wise woman who charmed burns, dispensed medicinal potions, and offered a shoulder on which to cry.

These wise women were anything but amateurs and, in fact, were often more skilled than the "doctors" that intermittently roamed the countryside. They knew the fundamentals of diagnosis and treatment, psychology, midwifery, and a host of related disciplines. Many of the cures that they discovered were later accepted and used by established medical practitioners.

———————

Not bound by religious conventions, these wise women freely mixed magic with medicine so as to strengthen the cure. Herbal medicines were compounded and applied with care and with an awareness of power.

Some of the wise woman's lore, both magical and medicinal, is herewith appended. Used together, they often affected a cure, or at least relief. (This is for first aid only. Serious conditions deserve attention from doctors or other appropriate healthcare practitioners.)

For Minor Burns

Medicinal: Immediately plunge the area into chilled (not icy) water. *Magical:* Blow thrice onto the area, saying:

Three ladies came from the east,
One with fire, and two with frost.
Out, fire; in, frost.

For a Cold

Medicinal: Drink ginger tea. Eat a sandwich made from sliced, raw onions on white bread.

Magical: Wear tiger's eye, garnets, rubies, and/
or carnelian.

To Stop Bleeding

Medicinal: Apply chopped or powdered dried yarrow flowers
to small cuts (like those caused by shaving). It acts as
a styptic.

Magical: Tie a knot in a red cord. Alternately, thrust the
knife or other implement that caused the cut deep
into the earth.

For an Upset Stomach

Medicinal: Drink two glasses of peppermint tea. Or, add
one drop pure peppermint essential oil to a large glass
of water and drink.

Magical: Place a penny in the navel.

To Ease Headache

Medicinal: Suck the juice from a bitter lemon. Vigorously
exercise. Smell fresh lavender. Do not lie down.

Magical: Write "Motter Fotter" on a piece of paper and have
the sufferer burn it in the company of three witnesses.

For a Toothache

Medicinal: Apply 1 drop oil of cloves to the afflicted root.
(See your dentist as soon as possible.)

Magical: Say "Galbes, Galbat, Galdes, Galdat," over the
sufferer. Or remove the stocking from the sufferer's
left foot, fold it crosswise, and place it beneath the
pillow at night.

Lunar Things

◇◇◇◇◇◇◇◇◇◇

Since antiquity, the Moon has cast an enchantment upon those who walk below it. Early magicians, who did much of the work of cataloging the natural world (a task which was later adopted by scientists), discovered many objects, places, and creatures intimately related to the Moon. This information was duly recorded in spellbooks and magical primers.

What follows is one such modern list of these "lunar things." This can be used as a guide to creating and performing magical rites empowered by the Moon.

Magical effects: Love, peace, tranquility, sleep, psychic awareness, prophetic dreams, healing, beauty, fertility, childbirth

Qualities: Moist, fertile, nurturing, loving

Rules: Women, the family, mothers, children, the tides, human emotions, gardening, Cancerians

Her Phrases and Magical Operations:
Waxing: All positive operations; beginnings
Full: All manner of rites
Waning: Destroying baneful energies, habits, and disease

Colors: White, silver, iridescent hues

Magical Tool: The Cup

Day of the Week: Monday

Number: 9 (or 3)

Season: Fall

Astrological sign: Cancer

Goddesses: Artemis, Diana, Hecate, Hina, Isis, Lucina, Selene

Gods: Sin, Nanna

Musical Note: B

Sense: Taste

Body: Stomach, breast

Activities: Swimming, sailng, bathing, washing, purifying, cleaning, dreaming, daydreaming, brewing, nursing

Clothing: Garments made of cotton or silk, white robes, white capes, bathing suits, silver jewelry, crescent Moon tiaras, necklaces and rings, white belts

Incense: 1 part frankincense, ½ part sandalwood, ¼ part myrrh, ¼ part white rose petals, a dash poppy seeds

Herbs: Camphor, cucumber, gardenia, jasmine, lemon, lemon balm, lettuce, lily, lotus, myrrh, poppy, pumpkin, sandalwood, seaweed, water lily; white flowered or night-blooming plants

Perfumes: Sandalwood, myrrh, rose water

Woods: Sandalwood, willow

Stones: Aquamarine, beryl, chalcedony, moonstone, pearl, selenite, quartz crystal

Metal: Silver

Symbols: Crescents, mirrors, seashells

Places Ruled: Oceans, beaches, brooks, pools, lakes, rivers, springs, shores, wells, bogs, canals, inns, kitchens, moats, the home, gardens, tubs, bedrooms, fountains, waterfalls, farms, ships at sea

Musical Instrument: Cymbals, gongs, sistrums, resonant metallic instruments

Tarot Suit: Cups

Foods: Coconut, crescent cakes, eggs, fish, ice cream, lemonade, shellfish, soup (most), vanilla pudding, white sauces, yogurt

Drinks: Lemonade, milk, kefir, champagne, white wines

Creatures: Baboon, bat, beaver, cat, chameleon, chicken, clam, cow, crab, elephant, fish (most), goose, hare, heron, horse, otter, owl, panther, rabbit, seal, sea turtle, sheep, shrimp

Fingernails and Magic

Fingernails are ruled by the Moon. Traditionally, nails are cut on the New Moon (or during the waxing Moon) in a fruitful sign (Cancer, Scorpio, Pisces) for longer, harder nails.

Starting with the little finger of the right hand, cut and file each fingernail in turn. This clockwise motion follows the apparent path of the Sun across the sky.

Trimming your nails on different days of the week brings different magical influences:

- **Monday:** Prophetic dreams, healing

- **Tuesday:** Arguments, conflicts

- **Wednesday:** Wisdom, travel

- **Thursday:** Wealth, abundance

- **Friday:** Love, friendships

- **Saturday:** Aging, sickness

- **Sunday:** Health

Hourglass Spells

◇◇◇◇◇◇◇◇◇◇

Hourglasses were once one of the main tools of timekeeping. Today they're rarely found, except in kitchens where they've been relegated to timing culinary pursuits. As devices that "keep time," and due to their unusual construction, hourglasses can be useful magical tools.

The following spells require an hourglass crafted from real wood (or metal) and genuine sand. Ideally, it'll run for at least one hour. If not, a smaller hourglass will do.

For the sake of clarity, the top portion of the hourglass (from which sand flows) is hereby termed the "sender bulb"; the bottom portion is the "receiver bulb."

The First Hourglass Spell
(To go into the past)

Sit comfortably before a table. Hold the hourglass in your talented (writing) hand and relax. Breathe deeply, calming your mind, your thoughts, your anxieties (if any).

Turn over the hourglass and set it on the table. It should be high enough so that you can look directly into the running sand and the receiver bulb. Gaze into the sand. As it slips from top to bottom, allow yourself to travel back in time. Your mind slips from the present into the past.

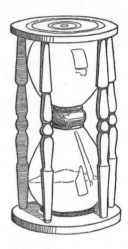

To facilitate this, say these or similar words in a slow, hushed voice:

> *Time now ... Time past ...*
> *Time runs ... Back fast ...*
> *Back to ... Time past ...*
> *Time now ... Is time past ...*

(This is an excellent method of reviewing other lives, retrieving "lost" information, finding misplaced objects, and so on.)

Let the movement of the sand send you backward to the proper moment. Know that you can instantly return to the present simply by saying, "Time now!"

The Second Hourglass Spell
(To send energy into an object)

Create a drawing or draw a rune that represents your magical need. Place this drawing (or, if necessary, a photograph) on a table.

Hold the filled receiver bulb of the hourglass in your talented hand. Visualize your need. Push personal power into the sand. See it glowing and humming with energy.

Turn over the hourglass. Set it on the object to be charged and leave the area. Let the sand do its work. As it runs from the top to the bottom of the hourglass, the energy that you've sent into the sand will be sent into the drawing or rune.

Repeat this entire procedure with the same drawing two more times. Afterward, bury the picture; burn it or quench it with water to release its potent energies to bring your need into manifestation.

Some "Witch" Terms

◇◇◇◇◇◇◇◇◇◇

Witch Balls: Glass spheres, usually silvered on the inside, that provide round reflecting surfaces. They were once placed in homes to drive away evil and were carefully dusted lest they lose their protective powers. Also known as "gazing globes"; in Victorian times they were placed in gardens.

Witch Blood: A concept created during the heresy persecutions that "witchcraft" ran in families and that a "Witch's" offspring were also Witches. This convenient theory led to the slaughter of entire families—who were quite innocent.

Witch Bottles: Bottles filled with a variety of substances and then buried or boiled on a fire to destroy the power of a supposed evil spellmaker.

Witch Boxes: Curious wooden boxes, filled with protective herbs and bizarre charms, with a top of glass. These were sold by Matthew Hopkins and other Witch-finders as devices that protected against the "evil" spells of Witches. Failure to buy such a box brought immediate suspicion and, potentially, arrest and execution for witchcraft. They were thus quite popular. This unholy racket continued in England for many years.

Witch Doctors: A derogatory Western term for persons who fill vital societal roles in many non-Western cultures. Such persons may be shamans, priestesses or priests, healers or magicians, psychologists, even scientists. The term has been banned from all serious sociological, anthropological, and ethnological studies.

Witch Hazel: A Native American tree (*Hamamelis virginiana*) long used for medicinal purposes. It has no direct, ancient associations with magic.

Witch Hunt: Originally, the search for "Witches" (i.e. supposed heretics). Since the 1950s, a general term for concentrated, biased, and absurd searches for enemies of all kinds, particularly in the realm of American politics.

Witch Mark: The supposed artificially created mutilation that Witch-finders sought on the bodies of the accused as proof of witchhood. In reality, these were normal blemishes and birthmarks. Since few bodies are perfect, many such marks were found—but they have nothing to do with witchcraft.

Witch Posts: These were created only in parts of Yorkshire and Lancashire in England. They were usually made of oak or rowan wood and were placed beside the fireplace to support the large hood that gathered the smoke and sent it up the chimney. Such posts were magically charged to guard the hearth and the home from evil.

Witch Stones: Stones bearing a natural perforation, used for protective magical purposes. Also known as "holey stones" and "hag stones."

Witch Tree: The rowan (or Mountain Ash; *Sorbus acuparia*), long used for protective magic.

Witches' Brew: Medicinal teas and magical brews made with plants and water. Today often used to refer to potent alcoholic beverages.

Witches' Familiars: Animal companions or pets, which may or may not lend their energies to magic.

Witches' Foot: An alternative word for "pentagram."

Witches' Hair: Often red or red-gold. This hair color was once believed to reveal that its bearer was a Witch.

Witches' Hour: A supposed time in the night marked by bats flying high and descending back to earth, during which magic is most effective.

Witches' Ladder: A length of rope or cord knotted in certain places. Feathers or herbs are usually attached between the knots. It was used for both blessing and cursing.

Witches' Thimble: Jimsonweed (*Datura spp.*).

Witching Hour, The: Midnight to 1 a.m., a traditional time for magical operations.

The Yule Tree

◇◇◇◇◇◇◇◇◇◇◇

The Yule Tree, once a Pagan symbol of rebirth honored at the Winter Solstice, has now been firmly entrenched in the contemporary Christian religious holiday that takes place at about the same time. Even so, the curious custom of bringing a tree indoors, decorating it, and honoring it during the month of December has never lost its Pagan origins, and it never will.

There are many stories of how and why this custom originated. Suffice it to say that the Yule Tree is a survival of earlier times, in which Pagan peoples, suffering through the winter, revered a living pine or fir tree as a symbol of the continuing fertility of the Earth. In other words, the Yule Tree represents the hidden seeds that will soon, with the coming of spring, burst forth into profuse growth, destroying the specter of winter and ushering in yet another cycle of fertility.

In magic, pine (and fir) is used for its purifying energies. Bringing a pine tree into the house during the shuttered month of December is an excellent method of magically freshening your home.

While many Christian customs have been layered onto this tradition, the true essence of Yule Tree rites is far older, far more earthy and magical. Here are some of these rites.

The Tree Itself

If you choose a cut tree, realize that the tree has given its life for your celebration. If you've chosen a living tree, know that it shouldn't be kept indoors for more than two weeks (in warm weather areas) and should be placed near a window to receive a bit of sunlight.

The Dedication

After you've brought it into your home and set it into place, hold your hands palms outward toward the tree and commune. Feel its life-energies still pulsing within it. (If it's a cut tree, thank the tree for its sacrifice.)

Now say these or words of similar intent:

O strong and noble, fragrant pine, That once shivered beneath the skies: Glimmer and shine now in my (our) home; Remind me (us) of the fertile loam That, far beneath the snow, still lies.

The Adorning

Yule Tree decorations are available in wide variety each year. Originally, apples, pears, walnuts, and other fruits and nuts were hung from the boughs, in further honor of the occasion: the rebirth of the Sun God at the Winter Solstice.

The shiny glass globes are modern representations of these earlier vegetative ornaments, and they can be used; so can real fruit. Apples can be hung from their stems, and small tangerines and oranges can be propped among the boughs. Blown-glass ornaments in the shapes of bunches of grapes, snow-frosted pine cones, and other natural shapes are usually available, and are a fine substitute for the real fruit. Garlands of cranberries and popcorn, of course, can also be made and used.

Avoid the use of plastic ornaments on the tree.

Lights are the modern (and safer) equivalent of the candles that once perched on sturdy boughs. They represent the Sun's glow, and can certainly be used if desired.

Decorate the tree as best as you see fit. When it's finished, stand back and admire it for its symbolism and for its real energies.

The Yule Tree's Passing

By tradition, all Yule decorations are removed by February 1. Usually, however, the tree is taken down long before this date. Even so, by the time the Winter Solstice has passed, a cut Yule Tree is usually dry, even if you've placed it in water. (If you've used a living tree, remove its decorations to return it to its original appearance. Keep inside, move to a porch, or place it outside. Give it proper care and you should be able to use it again the following Yule.) The tree's life force is ebbing even as the Sun grows in strength and glory.

After the decorations are removed, take a small bowl. Gently collect some of the dried needles from the tree, placing them into the bowl. When you've gathered a few handfuls, hold the bowl before the tree in both hands. Say these or similar words:

I thank you for your presence. Continue to shine in my life.

Hold the bowl up to the top of the tree, wait a second, then move the bowl clockwise around the tree's perimeter: from the top, down the right-hand side, to the trunk, up the left side, and back to the top once again.

As you move the bowl, feel the tree's fleeting energies streaming from every branch into the bowl. Transfer its powers into the needles that you've collected.

Place the gathered needles into an airtight jar. Once this has been done, take the tree to a recycling center (if one is available); use it for firewood (so that it can, once more, symbolize the Sun's energy); or mulch it (so that it can directly replenish the Earth's fertility).

Treasure the collected needles. During the winter, whenever the weather turns foul, or whenever you feel the need for refreshment, remove the top of the jar and inhale the needles' sweet, piney fragrance. Accept the energies of your Yule Tree until the waxing Sun melts the Earth's ice prison, spurring the rebirth of emerald fertility.

Treasured Sources

◇◇◇◇◇◇◇◇◇◇

The scent of herbal tea rises and mixes with the resinous aroma of incense. Candles and firelight create a bright glow in the room. A figure bends over a book, running a finger down a page, searching for an age-old ritual.

Suddenly, the magician's cat springs onto her lap. One errant paw flips over several pages of the book. The magician stares down at the page and smiles as she realizes that she's finally found the ritual for which she's been searching. The cat kneads. The magician pets her. The book seems to shine with energy.

Most practitioners of magic spend hours poring over old books. Classics of the hidden art line their bookshelves, waiting for use when needed. Years of searching have garnered a collection of time-honored works. The magician's reference library is, indeed, a valuable magical tool.

Most magicians have their own treasured sources of information, the books that have sparked their imaginations when searching for or devising new rituals, or altering others. Though each magician has her or his own favorites, I thought that I'd present some of mine to you.

Many of these books aren't magical texts, yet they contain much material of this nature. It was years before I realized that some of the best "magical" information is to be found in books of superstition and folklore, for both of these topics are solely concerned with the magic of past ages.

Some of these books are out-of-print and rather difficult to find, but most were printed within the last thirty or so years and may be available in new editions. Ask for them at used bookstores, or write to book search services for assistance in locating them.

And most of all, treasure these books for the knowledge that they contain.

Budge, E. A. Wallis. *Amulets and Talismans.* New Hyde Park: University Books, 1968. (A monumental collection of magical objects and their uses, from all parts of the world throughout history.)

Cirlot, J. E. *A Dictionary of Symbols.* New York: Philosophical Library, 1962. (A fascinating, worldwide

look at the meaning of symbols, including plants,
animals, birds, natural features, and much more.)

Elworthy, Fredrick Thomas. *The Evil Eye: The Origins and
Practices of Superstition.* New York: Julian Press, 1958.
(First published in 1895, this is a wondrous collection of
folk magical rituals: everything from magic nails to ritual
gestures to amulets and other protective devices.)

Fielding, William J. *Strange Superstitions and Magical
Practices.* New York: Paperback Library, 1966. (Despite
the sensationalized title, this is an excellent guide to
natural magic. Topics include rings, stones, fertility,
healing, love and weddings, protection, and much more.)

Frazer, James. *The Golden Bough.* New York: Macmillan,
1958. (Much magic is hidden among the dense pages of
this book, which was culled from the original 13-volume
work. Patience in reading it will be rewarded with an
amazing array of magical techniques.)

Kitteridge, George Lyman. *Witchcraft in Old and New
England.* New York: Russell and Russell, 1956. (Love
spells, image magic, herb rituals, divination, and
treasure-finding methods, culled from actual trial
records.)

Leland, Charles Godfrey. *Etruscan Magic and Occult
Remedies.* New Hyde Park: University Books,
1963. (A collection of Etruscan and Roman spells,

incantations, divinations, amulets, and other
wonders. Originally published in the late 1890s.)

Leland, Charles Godfrey. *Gypsy Sorcery and Fortune Telling.*
New Hyde Park: University Books, 1963. (Originally
published in 1891, this is a goldmine of Gypsy charms
and spells.)

Opie, Iona, and Moira Tatem. *A Dictionary of Superstitions.*
New York: Oxford University Press, 1989. (An instant
classic, this scholarly work records many magical practices,
including those related to the moon, eggs, cats, mirrors,
and much, much more.)

Radford, Edwin, and Mona A. Radford. *Encyclopedia of
Superstitions.* New York: Philosophical Library, 1949.
(A collection of British and Continental superstitions
and magical practices.)

Randolph, Vance. *Ozark Superstitions.* New York: Columbia
University Press, 1947. (Love charms, ghosts, divinations,
healing rituals, and more, culled from living informants in
Missouri and Arkansas.)

Thompson, C. J. S. *The Mysteries and Secrets of Magic.* New
York: Causeway, 1973. (A remarkable collection of magical
history and practice. Chapters discuss magical rings, ritual
perfumes, quartz crystal, numbers, ointments, and so on.)

The Splendor of Spellcraft

◇◇◇◇◇◇◇◇◇◇

Spells (simple magical rites) were once the province of all. Each family treasured and preserved certain magical remedies, mixtures, and charms that had been proven effective over many centuries. Such family spells were often written in small, leather-bound books and guarded from the eyes of strangers.

To perform such spells, there was no need for secret initiations, nor for noisome ingredients. The tools were those of any household: candles, herbs, pots and pans, mirrors, string and cloth. Short rhymes or strings of "mystic" words were another important tool.

Though a mischievous spell or two might have been included, the majority of such rites were devoted to securing love, protecting the home and its possessions, ensuring food (or its modern counterpart, money), and curing all manner of illnesses among both humans and animals.

Homely charms for halting the flow of blood, predicting the sex of unborn children, ensuring that churning was successful, blessing the fields for fine crops, guarding farm implements—these were some of the rites recorded in family books of magic.

———

Many of these old spells have now been gathered and published in books of folklore, folk beliefs, and magic. Yet many hundreds of others are still kept among the sanctity of the family and will never be revealed to anyone except blood relatives.

If you're not fortunate enough to have access to such a Magic Book, you have the opportunity to create one for your own family. Begin this magical operation on the night of the Full Moon, when potent energies are afoot on Earth.

Choose a small, unlined, bound book. Light a white candle. By its flame, draw a pentagram (five-pointed star, with one point up) on the first page.

On this page, beneath the pentagram, add the date of the book's creation, your mundane or magical name, the moon's phase and any other information that you see fit to include.

Hold it up before the candle (or to the Moon, if it's visible) and say these or similar words:

O stars, O sun,
O moon so bright,
Bless now this book
I've made tonight.

Now raise the book to the north, east, south, and west.

Copy at least one spell into the book on the night upon which you create it. In the coming months and years, you'll discover new spells, or others will share them with you. Faithfully copy them into the book. Create a type of code so that you can note whether they've been successful. Ideally, copy none into the book that haven't been proven effective.

Keep your book wrapped in white cloth, laid among moth-averting herbs (such as wormwood, rosemary, and cedar), or best of all, in a small, locked cedarwood chest.

Such a magic book can become a treasured heirloom, for it reveals the magical and spiritual nature of those who have created it, and, with its wisdom, the path of life can be smoothed.

Your magic book is an important tool in the splendor of spellcraft.

Herbs
and Food

The Magical Pantry

◇◇◇◇◇◇◇◇◇◇

Those of us called to the old ways usually set aside a special place in which to store our ritual supplies and tools. This place—the "magical pantry"—is an indispensable part of practicing natural magic.

For those romantics among us, this may be an intricately carved cabinet specially fashioned for this purpose. The wood may be of magically protective oak, hand-rubbed with a natural finish. Along its surface we might carve crescent Moons, planetary symbols, dragons, and runes. This cabinet usually stands in an honored place, away from prying eyes. Its flat top may even serve as a magical work place—the physical arena upon which nonphysical energies are urged into motion.

Usually, though, a magical pantry is simply any object in which the tools of magic are stored. It may be a chest, a large wooden box, a cupboard, or a drawer. Any object large enough to contain the necessary items is fine.

Among nonmagicians, a pantry consists of shelves of food, flour, honey, and other cooking essentials. A well-stocked pantry is an assurance of sustenance in the future.

Among magicians, a magical pantry is a vital tool for the practice of timeless rituals. It is a place of stored power. It is an assurance that the objects that may be needed in the future will be there, in one specific place, ready to be used.

You might wish to create your own magical pantry. It is a simple process. First, select any suitable container (such as those mentioned above). Remove any objects currently occupying it and find new homes for them. Ideally, the magical pantry should be used solely to house ritual implements and the consumable supplies of our art.

Fill a bowl with spring water. Add 1 teaspoon uniodized salt. Dip a cellulose sponge into the brine to wet it, squeeze it almost dry, and wash the container. Wipe every painted or stained surface lightly with the damp sponge, moistening it as needed. As you do this, sense its past energies dissolving in the salted water. Sense it being refreshed, prepared, cleaned.

In a small, dry bowl, mix together the following ingredients:

1 tsp. rosemary	1 tsp. sage
1 tsp. frankincense	1 tsp. cinnamon
1 tsp. sandalwood	

Blend well with your hands.

Next, light an incense charcoal block (not a barbecue incense cube!) and place in a burner. Sprinkle a pinch of the mixed incense onto the charcoal block and let it fume inside your future magical pantry until the smoke dies out. Add more of the mixture to the charcoal block. Cense your container for at least 13 minutes. (If you have no charcoal blocks, light a stick of quality sandalwood incense, push its nonsmouldering tip into a bowl of sand, and let it smoke inside the container until it extinguishes itself.)

Remove the censer and set aside. Your magical pantry is now ready to house its new occupants.

Before stocking its shelves, place a few objects into your magical pantry. These are never used for ritual. Instead, they watch over and guard your implements. These are:

Small mirror. It may be round or square. Affix to one of the walls inside your magical pantry. As you place it, visualize its surface reflecting away any negativity sent to it.

Small bag of salt. Tie up 2 tablespoons of uniodized salt into a white cloth, securing it with white string. Hold this in your hands, sending purifying energy into it. Place in the magical pantry. The salt is protective. It is also placed to ensure that your magical operations will be grounded, successful, and positive in their manifestations.

Bottle of power. Place three whole peppercorns in the bottle, saying:

Pepper for power.

Add five dried rose petals, saying:

Roses for love.

Carefully push seven pins into the bottle with these words:

Pins for protection.

Next, add nine threads to the jar, one each of the following colors: white, black, pink, red, orange, yellow, green, blue, and purple. Say:

Threads for manifestation.

Tightly secure the jar's lid and add it to your magical pantry.

That done, it's time to start stocking. The contents of your magical pantry will, of course, vary according to your interests and practices. If you're involved with herbalism, you'll have a lot of herbs. Here are some basics vital to virtually all practitioners of natural magic.

Tools

Incense burner. It may be of any design.

Knife. This is traditionally used to collect herbs and plants used in magic and for all cutting purposes. Some magicians favor silver as a metal that conducts energy, but choose one with a sharp edge for greater ease of use. (This knife is never used for sacrifices!)

Small bowls. You'll need at least three small bowls. These are used for blending herbs (such as the incense mentioned above), for containing various objects, and for other purposes. If you find a ceramic bowl with a black finish inside and out, it can be used to awaken psychic awareness. Fill with water and, by candlelight, stare into its depths until you know what you desire.

Cup or goblet. This is useful for toasting various deities (if your magic is spiritually oriented). Or, a ceramic mug or china teacup, used solely for the purpose of drinking ritual herbal teas (such as yarrow for love; peppermint for purification; rose for psychic awareness).

Tarot cards; rune stones; yarrow stalks and all other tools of divination.

Your **magical notebook,** in which you've recorded valuable rituals and bits of the old lore, as well as spells that have evolved themselves, and recipes for oils, incenses, baths, and other herbal mixtures. As the most valuable volume that you can own, your magical notebook should be kept in this special place.

Candleholders. These should be of glass, crystal, pottery, stone, or metal. It's best to clean them between uses. Immerse in a bowl of warm water until the wax has softened and can be pulled off. Rub with a cloth to complete the cleaning.

Glass bottles of various shapes and sizes. Canning and apothecary jars are ideal. Purchase them from import and cooking shops, or save bottles as you empty them.

Wash, sterilize, and store in the magical pantry until
needed.

Supplies

Herbs. A good selection to cover most needs would include
rosemary, sage, cloves, cinnamon, frankincense, sandalwood,
basil, yarrow, bay, thyme, and patchouli. Your stock will
grow. Replace jars with fresh herbs as you empty them.
Clearly label all jars.

Candles. Whether you use votive, tapers, or the glass-encased
seven-day variety, keep the whole spectrum of colors:
white, yellow, orange, pink, red, blue, green, and purple.

Stones. Keep water-smoothed pebbles from riverbeds (which
can be marked with magical symbols and carried) or
semiprecious stones such as amethyst, tiger's eye, carnelian,
rose quartz, aventurine, moonstone, and aquamarine.

Oils. You'll need true essential oils such as sandalwood,
lavender, black pepper, rosemary, ylang-ylang, rose
geranium, frankincense, benzoin, oak moss, and others,
as well as fixed oils for use as a base when mixing magical
blends: apricot, hazelnut, grapeseed, jojoba, olive,
sunflower, and almond.

Cloth. Natural fibers (cotton is always safe) in a rainbow
of colors are used for holding bundles of stones and
herbal mixtures.

Thread (cotton) or **yarn** (wool). Use for knot magic and
securing magical packages.

Salt. Sea salt may be preferred. This is invaluable for use in rituals of protection, prosperity, and purification.

Charcoal blocks. Obtainable from metaphysical and religious supply stores, they are necessary for burning granular incense. Or...

Stick incense. Buy only the finest that you can find. Keep frankincense and sandalwood in stock.

Other objects may certainly be included in your magical pantry. Some keep bottles of rainwater, collected during a heavy storm, for use in spells; a box of ritual jewelry worn only for magical purposes; bells; a crystal sphere, wrapped in cloth and preserved against damage in a small wooden box; and other ritual implements. And don't forget matches for use in lighting candles and incense. Small boxes of wooden matches are ideal.

Once you've prepared and stocked your magical pantry, it will become a valuable ally, a storehouse of power available for use. You'll never again search through endless drawers and boxes for the one item that you've misplaced. Everything will be there in its own place.

Keep some semblance of order in your magical pantry. Put herbs with other herbs, stones (perhaps wrapped in cloth bags and labeled) with stones. Candles should lie flat or hang suspended by their wicks from a shelf with tacks so that they won't warp and bend.

Place the items you use the most on the top shelf or in the most convenient spot. Nurture your magical pantry with care and it will nurture you on your magical journey.

Ritual Herbal Teas

◇◇◇◇◇◇◇◇◇◇

A cup of fragrant tea, a candle, and a moment of solitude can be especially relaxing. They can also create excellent opportunities for casting a spell on yourself, for herbal teas are delicious ways in which we can use the inherent powers of herbs.

Magically potent herbs release their energies into the water as they steep. When we carefully choose these herbs according to their powers, brew with ritual, and drink with intention, the simplest cup of tea can be a powerful adjunct to other forms of spellcasting.

For best results, follow these guidelines:

- Use about 1 tablespoon dried herb (or herbal mixture) per serving. Drink these teas in moderation.

- Use pure spring water if possible.

- Energize the tea before brewing by touching the herb (or herbs) and visualizing your need. Short chants are also appropriate.

- Warm the cup (or teapot) with hot water before pouring in the boiling water.

- Pour the boiling water over the herb in the cup (or teapot). Cover and brew until the water has released the herbs' energies.

- Let cool slightly, sweeten with honey (if desired), and enjoy.

Happy brewing!

Herbal Teas and Their Magical Energies

Alfalfa: Purification

Catnip: Peace (flavor with mint)

Chamomile: Love

Elderflower: Protection

Ginger: Protection (place a few slices of fresh ginger root in a cup with boiling water)

Hibiscus (Jamaica): Psychic awareness (drink cooled)

Lemon balm: Health

Lemongrass and rose: Psychic awareness (flavor with a dash of cinnamon)

Licorice root: Love and sex (boil licorice root)

Peppermint: Purification

Peppermint, spearmint, and thyme: Health

Rose hips and hibiscus: Love

Sage: Long life (sweetened with honey)

A Magical Healing Soup

◇◇◇◇◇◇◇◇◇◇

When you or a family member is feeling ill, gather together three green onions, one red onion, three bay leaves, a clove of garlic, and salt. Set a pot of spring (or bottled) water over the fire to heat.

As the water heats, chop the onions and garlic.

Sprinkle salt into the boiling water with these words:

With this salt
I now halt
Sickness and
Illness here

Add the chopped onions. Say:

Energize the
Atmosphere;
Send all illness
Far from here.

Smell the rising fragrance. Add the garlic with these words:

Garlic goes
In the pot.
Who is sick
Shall be not.

Smell the growing power within the kettle. Add the bay leaves while saying:

Leaves of bay,
Keep at bay
Illness today.

Continue heating for three minutes. Remove from heat and have the patient smell the magic "soup." Allow it to cool, uncovered.

When cool, strain and place in a jar. Add ½ cup to the bath water; add three drops of the mixture to a glass of water and drink, and pour the rest onto the ground to speed your healing.

Kitchen Witches

◇◇◇◇◇◇◇◇◇◇

Who would have thought thirty years ago that tens of thousands of American homes would be graced with images of flying Witches year-round, or that such Witches would be considered (even if not seriously) to be the bearers of good luck?

Few of us. Yet, within recent times, these images of elderly women have become a firm fixture in many kitchens. Dressed in Eastern European-style clothing and usually astride a broom, Kitchen Witches are advertised as having the power to prevent milk from spoiling and pots from boiling over.

These female symbols of power were originally made in Scandinavia and were crafted of natural materials. Though many today are made in Asia, thousands of craft fairs each year prove that Americans are also creating Kitchen Witches.

The popularity of such figures does indeed seem surprising, given the wicked image that witches have unjustly suffered for centuries. What could possibly be behind their popularity? I have a theory: Kitchen Witches may speak to their owners of the magical past, when elderly women were indeed "witches" of a sort.

Wise women, who were often combinations of midwives, herbalists, doctors, psychologists, counselors, psychics, and folk magicians, were an established part of European culture for centuries. Most of these women knew spells of love, protection, and health, and were frequently called upon for magical assistance by villagers.

In the days before "youth culture," the elderly were held in higher esteem for their wisdom and experience. Older wise women were naturally thought to possess more knowledge and have access to greater power.

For hundreds of years, wise women were allowed to openly practice their arts. Some called these women Witches, but at the time this was no crime, and the concept of Witches as evildoers had yet to be born. Female Witches were more akin to fairy godmothers: they were respected, not feared.

Soon, however, the great persecution of heretics began. Wise women were suddenly labeled as enemies of the dominant religion. Many were falsely accused of worshiping the devil and were executed without the niceties of a fair trial.

And so the wise women, who were healers, helpers, and doctors; who cured with spell and herbs; who birthed babies, counseled the depressed, and blessed the fields with fertility, came be to hated and feared through no fault of their own. This negative image of "Witch" was to remain until the present day in many parts of the world.

Since the Witch wasn't originally seen as evil, it seems likely that the modern-day popularity of the Kitchen Witch is based upon growing knowledge of the true nature of Witches, past and present. Kitchen Witches are depicted as flying as a sign of their magical abilities. The advanced age of most Kitchen Witches may indicate respect for the accumulated wisdom of the wise women.

Kitchen Witches seem to be both an apology to the wise women falsely accused of devil-worship as well as an unconscious yearning for a return to the past, when magic was an accepted practice and when the wise women helped all who came to them.

Foods of the Sabbats

◇◇◇◇◇◇◇◇◇◇

The four old festival occasions of pre-Christian European religions have been preserved today in the Wiccan Sabbats of Imbolc (February 1), Beltane (April 30), Lughnasadh (August 1), and Samhain (October 31).

Ritual usually begins at nightfall on the dates indicated, as this hearkens back to the time when the start of a new day began at dusk. After the seasonal observations are fulfilled, all join in a feast provided by the celebrants themselves.

Here are some unusual recipes for each of these four main Sabbats. Combined with other foods, they make hearty festival meals.

Imbolc

Imbolc is the time when, in Wiccan thought, the Goddess has recovered from giving birth to the God at Yule.

Imbolc Salsa

> 2 very large, very ripe tomatoes
>
> 1 small onion
>
> 1 to 2 canned Serrano chilies
>
> 1 tablespoon cilantro (fresh coriander leaves), finely chopped
>
> Salt and pepper to taste
>
> A dash sugar

Peel and finely chop the tomatoes. Finely chop the onion. Remove seeds from chile pepper(s) and finely chop. (Warning: two will make this quite hot). Place the first four ingredients into a bowl, season to taste, and let sit, refrigerated, for several hours. Serve cold with tortilla chips. (Serve with chili [vegetarian or con carne], beans, and rice.)

Beltane

Beltane marks the return of fertility to the Earth in late spring. Some Wiccans celebrate the marriage of the Goddess and God.

Beltane Herb Soup

1 small head lettuce

6 cups chicken stock

1 small bunch watercress

1 tsp. salt

1 cup sorrel

A dash black pepper

2 sprigs chervil

1 cup cream

3 tbsp. butter

1 egg yolk

Croutons

Shred lettuce; finely cut the watercress and sorrel, and chop the chervil. Cook the herbs in the butter for about 5 minutes until limp, but not browned. Add the stock, salt, and pepper. Cook for 30 minutes over medium heat. Add the cream and egg yolk. Stir until heated, but not boiling. Season to taste; add croutons.

(Serve with quiche, freshly baked bread, butter, and seasonal fruits.)

Lughnasadh

This is the occasion of the first harvest. Nature's fertility is dwindling as she prepares for winter and the hours of sunlight shorten each day.

Lughnasadh Corn

4 ears corn

½ tsp. salt

⅓ cup butter

2 tsp. sugar

⅓ cup onion, chopped

A pinch cumin

⅓ cup bell pepper, chopped

A pinch rosemary

¼ cup zucchini, chopped

1 large tomato, chopped

Husk and de-silk ears of corn. Cut kernels from ears until you've measured 2 cups. Place in pot. Add all ingredients except the tomato and cook over medium heat, uncovered, until butter has melted. Cover and cook on low heat for about 10 minutes. Add tomato. Cover and cook an additional 5 minutes.

(Serve with freshly baked whole-wheat bread, bean dishes, and blackberry pie.)

Samhain

Samhain is the fall festival in which Wiccans bid farewell to the God (represented by the Sun), who journeys beyond the western horizon.

Samhain Colcannon

2 pounds small potatoes

6 medium scallions (or 6 boiling onions)

4 cups green cabbage

4 tablespoons butter

½ to 1 cup warm milk

1½ teaspoon salt

Dash pepper

Pare and quarter potatoes. Peel and slice scallions into thin slices; cut in half. Finely shred cabbage.

Boil the potatoes until soft but not soggy. At the same time, boil the cabbage in a separate pot for about 9 minutes.

Drain the cabbage. Fry cabbage in a skillet in 2 tablespoons butter for 1 to 2 minutes; remove from heat. Cover. Let sit.

Drain the potatoes, return them to their pan, and shake over the fire until dry. Mash or whip potatoes. Add ½ cup milk and remaining butter and beat together. (More milk may be added if needed to create the proper puree-like texture.)

Add the cabbage and scallions to the potatoes; mix well. Season with pepper and salt. Serve at once.

Serve with a hearty stew, toasted bread spread with garlic butter (cream together ¼ pound softened butter with the pressed juice of 1 small clove of garlic), and a salad.

Ancient Herbal Spells

◇◇◇◇◇◇◇◇◇◇

O who can tell
The hidden powre of hearb,
And might of magick spell?
—Spenser

A simple wildflower nodding in the breeze, a root buried in the moist earth, fragrant leaves and pungent seeds: these are some of the oldest magical tools.

The connection between herbs and magic was forged long ago by the first power-workers. It was these brave persons who discovered the inherent energies that exist within plants of all types and devised methods for their use.

Herbal spells call upon the subtle power of a variety of plants and can be extremely effective, but magical rites such as those below will have no effect unless the magician senses, rouses, infuses, and moves the energies within the plants.

- If you have been robbed, collect sunflowers during the month of Leo and place them under your pillow. Sleeping on them, you will see the face of the thief in your dream.

- If you wish to keep snakes far from your property, plant the ground around your home with strawberries.

- Before sunrise on the first Tuesday after the New Moon, search for a four- or five-leafed clover. Keep this for luck in gambling.

- If you fear attacks by enemies, write your name on a fresh verbena leaf in red ink. Carry this leaf with you and your enemy will do you no harm.

- To keep evil spirits from the house, hang dried seaweed in the kitchen.

- To discover the future, take two acorns. Name one "yes"; the other "no." Place them in a basin of water and ask your question. The acorn that floats toward you indicates the answer.

- Grow myrtle on either side of the door to the house and love and peace shall ever remain within.

- Rub yourself with garlic or leeks before a confrontation for victory.

- To cure headache, grasp some freshly scraped horseradish in your hand.

- Gather the first anemone flower to bloom in the spring and carry it with you as a charm against sickness.

- Place thorny rose branches on the front doorstep to keep evil far from your abode.

- Consuming a bit of wild thyme before retiring will grant the diner a sleep free from nightmares.

- Burrs (those small seed capsules that adhere to clothing) are useful for improving the memory. Place some in a small bag and carry for this purpose.

- Keep money with cedar chips in a small box to attract yet more money.

- Eat borage for courage.

Shakespeare's Herbal Code

In the famous scene from *Macbeth*, three witches create a potion in order to conjure up the presence of their goddess, Hecate. The ingredients that they add to their cauldron aren't, in reality, as gruesome as may seem at first glance—they're herbs.

Shakespeare's works are dotted with herbal lore, and his Witches scene is an excellent example. Here are some tentative "translations" of the ingredients mentioned in the poem:

Fillet of a fenny snake: Fruit of a certain species of *Arum* known as "Snake's meat"

Eye of newt: Any of the "eye" flowers, such as daisies, bachelor's buttons, horehound, etc.

Toe of frog: Buttercup (*Ranunculus bulbosus*)

Wool of bat: Holly leaves (*Ilex aquifolium*)

Tongue of dog: Houndstongue (*Cynoglossum officinale*)

Adder's fork: Bistort (*Polygonium bistorta*) or Cuckoo-Pint (*Arum maculatum*)

Blind-worm's sting: Wormwood (*Artemesia absinthium*)

Lizard's leg: A creeping plant of some kind; perhaps ivy

Howlet's wing: A plant with fuzzy leaves, as some geraniums

Scale of dragon: Leaf of the Dragonwort (Tarragon; *Artemesia dracunculus*)

Tooth of wolf: Leaf from Wolfsbane (*Aconitum napellus*) or branch of Club Moss (*Lycopodium clavatum*)

Witches mummy: A plant used as a poppet (magical image); probably mandrake (*Mandragora officinalis*) or briony (*Bryonia spp.*)

Maw and gulf of the ravin's salt-sea shark: Seaweed

Root of hemlock, digg'd i' the dark: Hemlock (*Conium maculatum*)

Liver of blaspheming Jew: Root of Butcher's Broom (*Ruscus aculeatus*) ("Blaspheming Jew" was simply thrown in to "shock" his largely Christian audience)

Gall of goat: Honeysuckle (*Lonicera caprifolium*) or St. John's wort (*Hypericum perforatum*)

Slips of yew sliver'd in the moon's eclipse: Yew (*Taxus baccata*)

Nose of Turk: Turk's cap (*Lilium martagon*)

Tartar's lips: Some unidentified Chinese herb or food plant (assuming that "Tartar" is here used to describe the Chinese, as it was in the past; alternately, this might have been a plant known from Russia)

Finger of birth-strangled babe: Roots from a young dead tree

Tiger's chaundron: Could be Lady's mantle (*Alchemilla vulgaris*)

———

This seems to be a straightforward herbal spell. Put into other words, this formula might look like this:

Place the following into a cauldron of bubbling water:

Fruit of the arum	Ivy	Butcher's broom
Daisies	Geranium	Honeysuckle
Buttercup	Tarragon	Yew
Holly	Wolfsbane	Turk's cap
Houndstongue	Mandrake	Roots
Bistort	Seaweed	Lady's mantle
Wormwood	Hemlock	

While there's no proof that this was what Shakespeare had in mind, it's a good reminder that all is not as it seems in many old magical formulae—even those preserved in literature. (Of course, this would still be poisonous!)

Magical Container Gardening

◇◇◇◇◇◇◇◇◇◇

Magical Container gardens are delightful, if temporary, methods of using the inherent power of herbs. It takes little time to create one of these potent plots, and the energy spent is well returned.

———

General Directions: You'll need a two-foot wide, 8- to 10-inch-deep round clay flowerpot; potting soil or a good mix of earth, sand, and mulch, and lots and lots of little plants (seedlings or those sold in "pony packs" at nurseries across the country). Since this is an outdoor container that you'll be making, it's best to begin in the spring after danger of frost. Place small stones or broken crockery at the bottom of the pot to cover the drainage hole. Fill the container about one-third full with potting mix (or compost rich soil). As you pat it into place, say words such as:

Fertile you are; fertile you'll be,
This is my will; so mote it be!

Acquire the plants (recommended plants for different types of gardens are listed below). You'll need established seedlings or very compact small plants. Carefully remove these from their containers, ensuring that their roots aren't damaged. After arranging the plants on top of the soil according to the directions below, plant them while chanting. Add extra dirt as needed. Water well.

Once completed, water regularly. Visit your magical garden often to reap its subtle yet potent powers. Smell leaves and flowers; allow the plants to touch your soul. With a bit of love and attention, your magical container garden will give you months of enjoyment.

Happy planting!

———

Healing Garden: Plant four sages in a square and a fifth sage in the middle. Fill in corners with small carnations ("pinks"). As you plant, say:

Sage of Jupiter, pinks of the Sun;
Through you, healing shall be won.

———

Love Garden: Plant this garden at night by moonlight. Place a lavender plant in the center of the pot. Plant a ring of catnip around the lavender, then a larger ring of basil around the catnip. (Allow two to three inches between plants for future growth.) As you plant, say these or similar words:

> *Plants of Venus,*
> *Moon above,*
> *Draw now to me,*
> *Someone to love*

Protection Garden: Create this garden when the Sun is directly overhead. Visualizing a pentagram (five-pointed star) over the pot, plant one small aloe vera at each point. In the center, set a garlic plant. Chant these or like words as you plant:

> *This plot I make,*
> *This plot I sow;*
> *Guard me and mine*
> *Forever more.*

Gathering Magical Plants

◇◇◇◇◇◇◇◇◇◇◇

From the ancient books of magic come specific directions concerning the collection of plants to be used in magic. Early magicians followed these directions to ensure the plant's future ritual potency.

Some of these instructions are contradictory, depending on the source and their country of origin. For example, some writers state that plants should be gathered while facing the Sun, others that they should be collected before sunrise. Still, similarities are also present, and from these early records we can create a clear picture of magical gathering rites.

Generally, plants were to be gathered before sunrise, on the day of the week that ruled the plant.

Solar plants: Sunday
Lunar plants: Monday
Martial plants: Tuesday
Mercurial plants: Wednesday
Jovial plants: Thursday
Venusian plants: Friday
Saturine plants: Saturday

Additionally, the phase of the moon and the moon's sign were taken into consideration: roots and woods were collected in the waning Moon; fruits, flowers, seeds, and leaves during the waxing Moon. Certain plants were gathered at the Full Moon, and some (such as fern and mugwort) were collected on Midsummer or on other special days. May Day was another of these special herb collection times.

Nicholas Culpeper introduced astrological concerns. It was best, he wrote, if the planet that governed the plant was in the ascendant while it was being collected. (This was for the collection of medicinal herbs, but such information was also used by magicians). Culpeper also stated that plants should be gathered in those places where "they most delight to grow."

———

The direction that the gatherer faced was also of significance. Agrippa, in his *Three Books of Occult Philosophy* (English edition 1651), is quite explicit in this regard.

Herbs ruled by Saturn, Mars, and Jupiter, he wrote, should be gathered while facing east or south. Herbs governed by Venus, Mercury, and the Moon should be picked while facing west, for these plants "delight to be western." Solar plants are collected while facing the Sun, or the south.

Before leaving home to collect plants, the magician was instructed to be fasting, fresh from a bath and dressed in a white garment. She or he had to leave home "before speaking a word to any creature" that morning.

To prepare the plant for the collection, the magician often drew a circle on the ground around its trunk, usually with a magic knife or sword. With the wind at her or his back, the magician then used a nonmetal instrument to uproot the plant.

Under no circumstances should leaves, flowers, seeds, roots, bark, or wood be allowed to touch the ground after collection, as this would negate their magical effectiveness. The herb was carefully wrapped in cloth and taken home to be dried or immediately used in rite or spell.

Branches that were to be used as magical wands deserved special collection rituals. According to one old source, the magician must go to the tree before sunrise and face east, so that the branch would catch the first rays of the sun as it rose at dawn. If this rule wasn't observed, the wand made from it "would be good for nothing."

Some herbs required special gathering rites. Selago (club moss) was considered to be a very sacred plant. The magician approached the plant barefooted ("with feet washed"), dressed in white. Before the plant the magician laid an offering of bread and wine, then uprooted it. Club moss, thus properly gathered, could be used for protection or for mystic power.

Valerian was best collected on May 2. When gathering valerian, the following was recited:

> *I conjure thee, herb, for thou art worthy for all things in the world. In pleasance, in court before kings, rulers, and judges, thou makest friendship so great.*

The plant was collected, washed in human milk, wrapped in linen, and carefully taken home.

For some herbs, the actual act of gathering constituted the entire magical rite: to cure fever, the magician pulled up a nettle plant by the roots while stating aloud the name of the sufferer and the sufferer's parents.

Magicians today generally use different techniques. Ecological concerns and greater Earth-awareness guide us in our collection practices. We're conscious of the sacrifice that plants must make if we are to use them in magic.

We may still collect plants on certain days, in certain hours, and in certain phases of the Moon. But before collection, we attune with the plant, and explain what we're doing and why we're doing it. We may leave an offering at the plant's base. We avoid collecting so many leaves (or flowers) that the plant can't survive, and rarely remove an entire plant unless many others of the same type grow nearby.

Herbalists respect the Earth, and show this even when reaping its bounties.

> *The Ram, the Bull, the Heavenly Twins,*
> *The Crab and next the Lion shines,*
> *The Virgin and the Scales,*
> *The Scorpion, Archer, then She-Goat.*
> *The man that holds the Watering Pot,*
> *The Fish with glittering tails.*

(Old astrological poem from early almanacs describing the symbolic creature of each sign.)

Nature and Earth Power

Spices fragrant; spices enfold;
Bring me money, silver and gold.

A Primer in Natural Magic Spells and Rituals

◇◇◇◇◇◇◇◇◇◇

Natural magic is the branch of these occult (hidden) arts that was once public knowledge. It's a beautiful, loving use of natural energies to create positive change. Though it's been cloaked in secrecy for centuries, it's just as effective today as it was in the distant past. If you've never practiced natural magic before, here are the basics:

- Magic is the movement of natural energies to cause needed change.

- Magic isn't dangerous or evil.

- Magic is a genuine (but little understood) practice.

- Magic utilizes natural energies: those within your body, as well as those within plants, stones, symbols, and colors.

- You can feel this energy within yourself while exercising, walking up stairs, or performing other physical activities.

- You can stir up this energy at will by tightening your muscles.

- This energy is given purpose and direction by the nature of the spell, which may involve creating pictures or images in your mind.

- This energy is then released through relaxation of the muscles and by pushing it out toward its goal, which may be a candle, a stone, an herb, a tub of water, or even the atmosphere.

- Magic is used for positive reasons.

- Magic is never used to cause harm.

- Magic isn't used for others without their permission.

- Magic can always be used to help yourself (indeed, this is the best reason for using it).

Does this seem simple? It is. Does this seem complex? It is. Why are these two statements seemingly contradictory? Find the answer in the practice of natural magic.

Natural magic is a precious legacy that earlier generations have given to us.

Spells and Rituals

The following spells can be performed by anyone, anywhere, as long as a need exists. These spells address common needs: money, love, and protection. They're nonreligious, require little specialized equipment, and can be surprisingly effective. For maximum results, perform one spell at a time. If you have many needs, decide which is the most important and concentrate on that.

Perform these rites with the proper attitude: expect results. Realize that most magical rituals must be repeated several times. Know that magic isn't supernatural, and its effects don't materialize before your astonished eyes in a supernatural way. The more you practice natural magic, the more aware you'll become of its possible positive applications in your life. Natural magic is a powerful tool of positive change.

The Cornucopia Spell (to attract needed money)

Items Needed: a wooden, ceramic, or glass bowl; 3 tablespoons ground cinnamon; 3 tablespoons ground cloves; a smaller, nonmetallic bowl or cup.

Wash the bowl well. Dry. Place it somewhere in the house where it can remain undisturbed for at least three weeks.

Measure the ground spices and pour them into the smaller bowl. Mix well using your fingers, while saying in a low voice, with great intent, as you tighten the muscles in your fingers, arms, and shoulders:

> *Spices fragrant; spices enfold;*
> *Bring me money, silver, and gold.*

Repeat this chant at least five times while mixing the ground cinnamon and cloves. Feel the energy that vibrates within the spices.

Place the small bowl beside the larger bowl. Fish out a few coins from your pocket or purse. Place them into the larger bowl. Then take a pinch of the powdered spices and sprinkle this on top of the coins while repeating the "Spices fragrant" chant. See a stream of money-attracting energy beaming out from the bowl. At least once a day, or more often if you wish, add a few coins to the money cornucopia, sprinkle on a pinch of the spices, and say the chant. Continue this until the spices are gone. Money will come to you.

(Note: Don't remove any of the coins that you've placed in the bowl. Allow them to rest there, adding their own money energies to those of the spices. When you've used up the spices, remove the coins and spend them in whatever way you wish. If desired, recharge the spices with the above chant, wash the dish, and restart the spell.)

The Love Stone (to attract love)

For this ritual you'll need nothing but yourself and your deep desire for a loving relationship.

Go to a spring, visit the beach, or walk beside a river or a lake. A dry riverbed (in desert regions) is also fine. Let a stone find you (don't look for one). One stone, and only one stone, will be suitable: it will be small enough to fit into your hands and will probably be smooth.

Once you have the stone, hold it loosely between your palms. See yourself enjoying a loving relationship, not with

"Joe Smith," "Jessica Thompson" or a specific person, but with someone who, perhaps, you haven't yet met.

Build up an image in your mind. See the two of you having a quiet dinner, listening to music, and enjoying mutual interests. Make this picture real in your mind.

Now press your palms tightly together against the stone. Pour this energy into the stone. Force it from your palms. The rock is a sponge—a solid yet permeable sponge—sopping up your desire for a loving relationship.

When you've forced out as much energy as you can, transfer the stone to your talented hand (your writing hand) and throw it into the spring, the ocean, the river, lake, or dry lakebed. Fling it from you, knowing that your energy goes with it.

As it contacts the water (or the sand), it releases the energy that you've lent it. Forces will be set into motion. Be active. Someone, eventually, will find you.

The Flaming Key (a house protection rite)

Items Needed: a duplicate key to your house (that you won't need to use at any time); a red candle; a book of matches.

At dawn, or as near to sunrise as possible, take the key, the candle, and the matches to the inside of your front door. Realize that the key can open or shut off entrance to your home. Realize that it can stop both physical as well as non-physical intruders.

Set the key and the matches down. Hold the candle between the palms of your hands. See your home as a safe, guarded, protected place—a place of sanctuary and security. See it as a fortress against unwanted persons or energies.

Say these or similar words:

Guard this house
To the core.
Guard it now
From roof to floor.

Pour this protective energy into the candle. Feel it rushing from your hands into the taper. Do this until you feel like you are about to burst.

Transfer the candle to your left hand, if you're right-handed. (If left-handed, to the right). Still holding the candle, pick up the book of matches with your free hand and strike one of the matches. Light the candle's wick.

Set down the book of matches. As the candle's flame rises, say:

Guard this house,
Guard it well.
Guard the house,
By this spell.

Hold the candle before the door for at least a minute. Sense its energies stirring and rising through the flame as the wax melts.

Now pick up the key, the magical instrument which will protect your place of residence. Holding it in your left hand (if right-handed), smash the key down onto the candle's flame, quenching it and, simultaneously, transferring all the candle's power into the key.

Set aside the candle. Touch the key to the front door's lock and say:

Guard well this house,
O flaming key.
This is my will,
So mote it be!

Place the key somewhere inside the house near the front door (perhaps under the rug or carpeting). It will guard your home so long as it's never used to open the front door.

Trees as Tools of
Psychic Awareness

◇◇◇◇◇◇◇◇◇◇◇

To be performed on any windy spring or summer day in which leaves still dangle from the trees:

Go to a safe, lonely place where there's little chance of being disturbed.

Sit or lie comfortably beneath a tree bearing large leaves. Close your eyes for a few moments, breathing deeply, calming yourself for the coming rite. Clear your mind.

When ready, open your eyes. Look up into the moving leaves, or at the ever-changing shadow patterns created by sunlight shining through them.

Lose yourself in the ever-moving spectacle of twisting leaves or shadows. Don't study them; simply be with them. Allow the wind's movement to lull your conscious mind and to awaken your psychic consciousness.

As you feel your consciousness slipping away, ask your question, or simply open yourself to the answer.

Unbidden thoughts will arise from your subconscious mind. Among them may be that which you seek. Listen to them—and remember.

After your rite, jot down the important images that you received during your meditation. Think about them and determine if any are applicable.

Repeat on any appropriate day.

Weather Omens

◇◇◇◇◇◇◇◇◇◇

Farmers, sailors, and most people throughout the world have always been dependent upon the weather. Before the invention of weather satellites, animals, plants, and a number of other things were observed for hints of approaching storms, the end of frost, calm days, and other weather patterns.

Recent research indicates that many of these older methods are far more reliable than are the modern forms of applied weather forecasting technology. Weather omens are often contradictory, but all have been observed in their day in various locales. These weather omens have largely been gathered from European and American sources:

Storms

- Blue flames in the fire
- Cats sitting with their backs to the hearth
- Clovers contracting their leaves
- Horses standing in a group facing away from a hedge
- Unusually busy ants
- Marigold flowers not opened before 7 a.m.
- Swallows flying low
- Spiders destroying their webs

Rain

- Ants hiding themselves
- A rainbow in the afternoon
- The scent of flowers growing stronger
- Cats sneezing
- Dogs eating grass
- Owls hooting
- Pitcher plants opening wider
- Bees remaining in their hives
- Spiders deserting their webs for other shelters
- Smoke refusing to go out the chimney

- Bats flying into the house
- Snakes hunting food

Good Weather

- Cows lying on high ground
- Bats flying at twilight
- Squirrels eating nuts in the trees
- Robins singing on a barn
- Larks flying high
- Spiders creating webs in the morning
- Wind blowing from the west
- Goats leaving their homes during a rain

Other Weather Indicators:

- **Heat:** Watercress patches steaming in the evening
- **Cyclones:** Migrating birds flying wildly in the air
- **Earthquakes:** Dogs barking

Earthquakes

Though earthquakes are occasionally devastating; most are of minimal magnitude and cause no damage. In fact, sensitive equipment records thousands of earthquakes each day that aren't noticed by humans.

In their less severe forms, earthquakes were once considered to be omens. The omen was read from the time of day at which the earthquake occurred. An old divinatory poem reads:

There are things
An earthquake brings:
At nine of bell
They sickness fortell;
At five and seven
They betoken rain;
At four the sky
Is cleared thereby:
At six and eight
Comes wind again.

Bird Charms

◇◇◇◇◇◇◇◇◇◇

Gathered from a variety of sources, these charms, consisting of representations of birds or of their feathers, all rely upon the intrinsic magic possessed by the creatures themselves.

(If you plan on using feathers as charms, use only those that have naturally fallen. Killing any bird for its feathers is not only cruel and senseless, it's also illegal in many places.)

Dove: Carry the feathers as a love talisman.

Eagle: Some peoples of North America once wore an eagle feather to drive off evil. Today, possession of any raptor feather (eagles, hawks, falcons, owls, or vultures) is punishable by law in the United States, with some exceptions. However, a representation of an eagle can be worn for protection.

Goose: The feathers draw love.

Hawk: See above. Images of hawks are carried on ships and airplanes for protection against accidents during travel.

Ostrich: The feathers may be carried to learn the truth of a matter.

Owl: See above. An image in the shape of an owl is worn or carried to instill wisdom, often during examinations.

Seagull: Use the feathers in travel charms.

Swallow: A brooch fashioned to resemble flying swallows is worn to bring good fortune.

Wren: The feathers, carried or worn, guard against drowning while at sea.

A Snow Spell

⬦⬦⬦⬦⬦⬦⬦⬦⬦

Spells—rituals—are often tools of self-transformation. The following ritual utilizes one physical manifestation of Water: snow. This is, by necessity, a winter ritual. Winter can be a time of stifling isolation from nature. Though I live in sunny San Diego, I designed this ritual during a winter trip to St. Paul, Minnesota. The remarkable nature of snow (a liquid in a fairly solid form) is utilized to represent an existent negative condition or habit. If snow isn't available, shaved or crushed ice can also be used.

Remember, such rituals are valuable psychological boosts, but when energy is truly transferred, magic is afoot and changes occur through means not readily explained.

To Be Rid of a
Negative Condition or Habit

When you've decided to no longer allow a harmful habit or condition to control your life, perform this ritual.

Dress warmly. During the day, go outside with a small, cereal-sized bowl. Fill the bowl with fresh, white snow. Pack it tightly, level it off with your gloved hand, and rush back inside.

Remove your cold-weather clothing and your gloves. Place the bowl of snow on a table. Standing over it, hold your hands, palms down, over the bowl. Say:

> *Crystal white,*
> *Crystal snow;*
> *Help me fight*
> *The evil blow.*

Visualize (see in your mind's eye) the habit within the snow. See the negative condition as existing within the snow. Know that it, its causes, and the power that you give it, are in the snow.

Transfer the negative energy through your palms into the snow.

Now, pour ½ handful of rock (de-icing) salt into your right hand (if right-handed; if left, use the left). Looking down at the white substance, sense its purifying, cleansing energies.

Still visualizing your negative habit in the snow, sprinkle the salt over the snow until you've completely covered its surface. Say:

White on white,
Salt on snow;
Fight your fight,
Evil go.

Next, take any small stone no more than 1½ inches in length or width. Hold this in your dominant hand. Visualize freedom from your negative habit or condition. See yourself free from its grip. Visualize your life without this harmful condition. Feel the power that you possess to break the chain.

After a few moments, gently place the stone on the surface of the salted snow. Say:

Rock on salt,
Salt on snow;
Evil halt;
Evil go.

Sit before it, staring down into the bowl. Watch. Sense. Visualize the purifying potency of the salt destroying your habit, its causes, and the power that you have been giving it.

As the snow melts, release all connections that you have with the habit. Visualize and feel your unconscious desires melting, dissolving into a sea of apathy, an ocean of disinterest, a surging river of purification.

When the salt has melted the snow, remove the stone, pour the water outside of your house (away from any plants that may sleep beneath the blanket of white), and return inside.

Wash the bowl and the stone. Put away in a safe place until the next day. Repeat the entire ritual for nine days. Visualize. Use your support groups. And just do it!

The Magic of May Dew

The fair maid who, the first of May
Goes to the field at break of day,
And washes in dew from the hawthorn tree,
Will ever after handsome be.
—Traditional

Dew forms mysteriously on cool, cloudless, windless nights, covering trees, bushes, and even animals. This pure liquid is thought to be the quintessence of water. Its unexplained appearance led it to be used in many spells and rituals.

Dew collected in May is thought to be especially powerful. As recently as the 1800s, whole towns in England would be up well before dawn. By 4 a.m. persons scurried around with small containers, collecting dew from leaves, herbs, and grass.

Though all dew is considered to be magical, that collected on May 1 has always been thought to be the most potent for both magical and medicinal purposes.

Here is some of May Dew's magic:

Washing the face and hands with the dew imparts luck. Applied to the face, it also safeguards it from wrinkles, blotches, and freckles. This "fine cosmetic" was thought to preserve youth and was widely used to enhance beauty (especially dew collected from the hawthorn, as mentioned in the above traditional rhyme).

Unmarried women tossed some of the precious liquid over their shoulders in order to attract "good husbands," while anyone could wash their hands in May Dew to attract the best of fortune throughout her or his life. It was also a powerful addition to love mixtures.

This liquid had its medicinal uses as well. May Dew gathered from fennel and celandine was used to treat sore eyes, while walking on dew-damp grass was thought to cure gout as well as rheumatism. In Spain and France, many persons rolled naked in the dew on May 1 to guard themselves against diseases of the skin and rheumatism for one year.

The liquid was snuffed up the nostrils to cure vertigo, and chemists and witches alike added May Dew to medicinal mixtures. Babies were "strengthened" by placing them on dew-covered grass on May Day morning (or by washing them with a bit of dew).

In the Isle of Man, women washed their faces with May Dew to protect themselves against evil spells, and in Eastern Europe, farmers bathed their cows with this liquid to preserve them against harmful charms.

The Magic of Shells

◇◇◇◇◇◇◇◇◇◇

A wave washes up, spilling foam onto the glistening sand.

Within the surging water tumble treasures from the deep. As the wave recedes, these jeweled wonders sit patiently on the sand, waiting the next wave or an interested collector.

Many children gather shells. Many adults, too, have traveled widely to garner vast collections of these fascinating objects, and are willing to pay $800 and more for an extremely rare shell, such as the exquisitely beautiful golden cowrie.

Few children, and even fewer adults, however, know of the hidden powers contained within seashells. Long used in magic and religious rituals, shells continue to hum with oceanic power, and can be utilized to bring love, money, protection, good fortune, and many other energies into their finders' lives.

For years I've wandered up and down Pacific, Atlantic, and Gulf of Mexico beaches, searching for treasures that have washed up from the ocean's depths. Walking beside the water breathing in the crisp, saline air is an invigorating and healing experience. This wonderful exercise holds yet another possible benefit: finding a magical object or two.

Though different types of shells are found in various parts of the country, certain forms are widely distributed, or can be purchased in specialty stores or craft shops.

Because destroying life is against all magical principles, use only those shells that you find without living creatures inside. Many times I've had to leave a shell on the beach when I discovered that its original occupant was still in residence.

To Use Shells in Magic

Charge the shell by holding it between the palms of your hands. See in your mind's eye the effect that you wish the shell to make: protection, love, purification, banishment of negative thoughts or illness, peace. Push and pour out this mind-and-body generated energy into the shell.

Once the shell has been magically charged, you have many options. You can toss the shell into the sea to release its powers; carry it with you or wear around your neck (if the shell is small enough); place on an altar near candles; fill or surround it with herbs and stones. You're limited only by your imagination. (For recommended candle colors, stones, and herbs, see the table at the end of this article.)

Here's a small sampling of these gifts from the sea.

Cowries are found throughout the world in warmer waters: off the coasts of California and Mexico; in Polynesia, Micronesia and Melanesia, India, China, and elsewhere. A certain form of cowrie was used as money in China as early as 600 BCE. They were soon heavily traded around the globe as a valuable commodity. Some contemporary religions use a cowrie shell to represent the Goddess in sacred rituals, and among certain sects of Yoruban religion, cowries are a highly prized divinatory tool. They've also been used as symbols of royalty and of warriors. Magically, cowrie shells are charged and used to attract money energies.

Oysters, long eaten to promote sexual arousal, have another use: a piece of the shell is carried to promote good fortune. Alternately, charge an oyster shell to find someone with whom to share a loving relationship.

White "clam" shells (bivalves) are common on beaches throughout the world. Some species grow to be the largest shells (the famous "giant clam"). Magically, they're charged and used in rites of purification.

Cone shells, of which there are many varieties, can be found on beaches off California, Mexico, the Gulf States, the Atlantic side of Florida, and elsewhere. Though the creature that inhabits them can be quite dangerous when alive, the shell itself is useful for protective rituals.

Abalone shells are uncommon but can occasionally be found on the beaches of California, Mexico, and Hawaii. The Navajo used water-filled abalone shells in rain-producing rituals. During many summers at Laguna Beach, California, I collected dozens of tiny abalone shells that had washed up on secret beaches. The iridescent, prismatic colors of the inner shell make them perfect for all magical purposes. Fill them with herbs or stones; anoint them with oils; carry or wear a small shell after charging it with power.

Left-handed whelks, found in Gulf of Mexico waters, are fine instruments of making dramatic changes in your life, such as halting negative habits. Charge with power as you visualize yourself making this change. (Use the herbs, stones, and candle colors listed under "purification" below.)

Conches, which are so popular in Florida, are fine, large, orange shells with a flaring pink lip. Charge a conch with love-attracting energies and put it in a place of importance in your bedroom.

Olive shells, found in Gulf of Mexico waters, are soothing shells that can assist in healing. Charge and place the shell near a blue candle.

Candles, Stones, and Herbs

Love: Pink candles. Stones: Rose quartz, greenn troumaline, amethyst. Herbs: Lavender, rose petals, basil.

Protection: Red candles. Stones: Obsidian, carnelian, garnet. Herbs: Black pepper, hyssop, juniper.

Purification: White candles. Stones: Aquamarine, calcite. Herbs: Chamomile, cedar, fennel.

Healing: Blue candles. Stones: Bloodstone jade, lapis lazuli. Herbs: Sage, eucalyptus, fennel.

Money: Green candles. Stones: Aventurine, olivine, bloodstone. Herbs: Ginger, cinnamon, clove.

Spells

◇◇◇◇◇◇◇◇◇◇

Spells are the means by which folk magicians gain control of their lives. Such rituals are designed to release energy within ourselves as well as to arouse the powers that naturally reside within certain objects.

The three following spells utilize different tools and have differing goals, and yet all three share a common thread—the underlying power of nature and our ability to tap into this energy during rituals.

Remember to visualize, to create pictures in your mind of your spell's goal. Without doing this, you're merely playing with stones, mirrors, and herbs.

A special ritual has also been included which allows the magician to tap into the energies of midnight prior to performing any type of spell.

Nutmeg and Mirror Spell for Money

You will need a nine- to ten-inch square mirror, a few teaspoons of finely ground nutmeg, a candleholder, one green candle, and matches.

After sunset, assemble the necessary items on a desk, table, or altar. Turn off all artificial lights. Sit and clasp the candle between your palms and sense its money-attracting energies. Push it into the holder and light it.

Place the mirror, reflecting side up, on the table at least a foot from the candle. Stare down into your reflection by the candle's flickering light. Say something like this:

Mirror of silver, glass, and light;
Bring me prosperity tonight!

Gaze into your reflection, seeing yourself as a financially stable person. Allow yourself to visualize how you'll look and feel when you have the money that you need.

Still staring down at and into your reflection, sprinkle the ground nutmeg over the mirror. Be sure to cover most of its reflective surface. Smooth it with a finger until the spice is evenly dispersed. Close your eyes, lower your head slightly, and sniff the exotic aroma. Say these or similar words:

Nutmeg, nutmeg, sweet as honey;
Fill my life with needed money.

Feel the spicy odor energizing your body, transforming you into a financially stable person. Open yourself to receiving additional funds. Visualize yourself as a prosperous person.

Open your eyes. Look down at the herb-covered mirror. Using the index finger of your writing hand, draw a six-inch square on the mirror through the ground nutmeg, carefully creating a narrow box of silver that shows through the spice.

Next, push the same finger into the center of the mirror. Move it in small circles, slowly pushing outward until a round section of the mirror has also been cleared of the nutmeg.

Look at your face in the mirror (adjust your distance from it if necessary). Hold both hands palms downward on either side of the mirror, strongly visualize extra money as already being a part of your life, and say these or similar words:

Magical glass and nutmeg rare;
Money will fly here through the air.
Prosperity will come to me:
This is my will, so mote it be!

Sit there staring into the mirror, smelling the nutmeg and visualizing.

After a few moments (you'll know when), carefully pour the nutmeg from the mirror onto a sheet of paper. Fold up the paper to trap the spice inside it and place in an airtight jar. Dust off the mirror with your hand. Pinch out the candle's flame (or use a snuffer). Store the nutmeg, the mirror, the candle, and its holder in a safe place until the next night.

Repeat seven nights in a row.

A Midnight Chant
for Increased Power

(To be performed prior to any midnight ritual)

For best results, go outside into the inky void of night about five minutes before midnight. Stand with your legs slightly spread. Raise your arms above your head. Feel the soothing yet potent energies of the night filtering into your consciousness, brushing against your body, tugging at you.

Take three deep breaths, listening, waiting. Gaze up at the darkened sky. If the Moon or clouds are present, watch them. Calm yourself. Prepare yourself.

Open your consciousness to the living reality of night. Let it enfold you. Feel the embrace of its timeless energies. Sense them transforming you.

After five minutes or so, say the following words in a hushed, whispered voice to bring the energies of the night within you:

> *O stars whirling through the sky above;*
> *O power hiding from the light;*
> *O black curling on the darkened land;*
> *O secrets biding in the night*
> *O ebon treasures of the drowsing Earth;*
> *O haunting forces of the deep;*
> *O misty measures of the circling sky;*

O daunting splendors that you keep;
Come to me with your shadowed kiss!
Fill me with your mystic power!
Come to me with your arcane might!
Be here at this midnight hour!

Let your arms fall to your sides.

Do not be afraid. The cool energies of the night cannot and will not harm you. Willingly accept them. Drink in the power that the stars, the sky, and the Earth have given you. Feel the remarkable change that has occurred within you.

Show your appreciation by facing north and raising your hands in honor. Repeat this at the east, south, and west. Facing north again, lift your hands far above your head, reaching into the night itself, then bend and touch them lightly to the ground before your feet.

The time has come. The power of midnight vibrates within you. Positive spells of all sorts may now be done—energized by the might of the darkness.

A Protective Amulet

This must be performed during the day when the Sun's protective rays flood the Earth with light. It is designed to protect yourself, your home, and your loved ones.

Draw a bath. Add ½ cup baking soda and ½ cup warm beer to the water. Bathe in this purifying mixture. Afterward, dry yourself and dress in clean clothing (a robe is fine).

(If you have no bathtub, pour the baking soda into a washcloth. Soak this with the beer. Rub your body with the sodden washcloth following a shower.)

Light sandalwood or frankincense incense. Assemble the following items at your altar or on any table:

A bag made of white cloth

1 dried clove of garlic

3 juniper berries

5 dill seeds

7 bay leaves

9 rosemary leaves

1 fossilized shark's tooth

1 small white stone

1 small piece of obsidian

1 small quartz crystal

1 lodestone (magnetite)

2 polished tiger's eyes

1 hematite

Place each of the items individually in the bag. As you add each one, say:

Strength to my protection!

When you've completed this, hold the bag between your hands. Press your palms against it and say these or similar words:

Garlic and berries; leaves and seeds;
Quartz and fossil; magnet that feeds;
Tigers' eyes and the stone that bleeds;
Crystals strong and magical weeds;
Guard me and mine and all who roam
Within this place, this house, our home;
Surround us as a shining dome,
Protect us all from roof to loam.
I charge you now: your power's free!
This is my will; so mote it be!

Visualize as you hold the bag. See it emanating a brilliant whitish-purple light that drives back all negativity, that protects your home and all those who reside within it.

Repeat the chant two more times. After the third, tie the bag closed with red yarn or cording. Take the bag outside into the Sun. Let its own light and energy further charge your protective amulet. When it has been warmed, bring it back inside.

Put the protective bag in a secure spot in your home, preferably near the front door.

Maneki-Neko, the "Good Luck" Cat of Japan

◇◇◇◇◇◇◇◇◇◇

Virtually every home and business throughout Japan displays a small ceramic image of a cat with one paw upraised. These "beckoning cats," known as Maneki-Neko, are reverently regarded as bringers of good luck, prosperity, and health. Such cat images are also found in cemeteries and in temples in Japan. Maneki-Neko is the most popular all-purpose charm used in Japan today.

These cats are found in a variety of sizes, from two inches to about eight inches in height, and even larger. Some are hand-painted and others bristle with jewels. The most important aspect of the beckoning cat, however, is its color, which dictates its magical effects.

The white cats invite good luck of all kinds and are the most commonly seen form. The black ones protect against disease and all health problems, while the lustrous gold cats open the door to prosperity. The raised paw invites in the energies.

Such cat figures are sometimes seen in Japanese-owned businesses in the United States, but in Hawaii they're found in the majority of stores and homes. From a cramped, pungent vegetable market in Honolulu's Chinatown to a luxurious jewelry outlet within sight of Diamond Head, Maneki-Neko sits near the cash register, drawing customers and business.

The luck-bringing qualities of Maneki-Neko are somewhat obscure. She was an attractive female cat who lured disobedient children into the clutches of an old sorcerer, To-kai-di, who speedily ate the transgressing kids. This would certainly give her attracting powers, but how she came to be associated with luck, money, and good health remains unclear.

Still, cats have played a long and important role in Asian history. Though some frightening felines have wandered through the beliefs of Japan, China, and Korea, most of these cats have been the beneficial guardians of humans.

Cats were highly regarded on Japanese ships. A cat of three colors (red, black, and white) was thought to possess the ability to predict storms while at sea. When a storm approached, the cat climbed up the mast and guarded the ship from the souls of those who had died at sea and endlessly wandered on the waves.

A few paintings of cats have been claimed to have the power to drive away rats and mice from the temples and homes in which they're placed, even if a genuine cat isn't also present.

Perhaps the most touching cat story of old Japan concerns the aged fish seller. In the early 1800s, he became ill and, because he couldn't work, soon was destitute. A cat assumed a human form and gave the fish merchant two gold coins in thanks for the man's years of unsparing kindness: he never failed to give the cat a few scraps of fish when he called at the cat's owner's home. Though the cat was unthinkingly killed by its owner for stealing gold coins, the owner, upon hearing the fish merchant's tale, buried the cat in a temple and gave it the honors it deserved.

In stories such as these, and in the Maneki-Neko, the cat still holds a firm place of honor in Japan.

Ancient
Cultures and Lore

Magic in Hawaii

◇◇◇◇◇◇◇◇◇◇

An ancient temple lies twelve bumpy miles from Highway 11 on the Big Island of Hawaii. Here, on this isolated spit of land known as Ka Lae, is Kalalela Heiau. The fishermen who still work these waters leave offerings to the Hawaiian deities on the lava stone structure.

Several years ago, the Kapiolani Rose Garden, near Diamond Head on the island of Oahu, was experiencing a rash of thefts. Tourists were stripping off the blooms and whole rose bushes were being spirited away. Charles Kenn, a renowned *kahuna*, was called in to protect them. The thefts stopped.

Many students of *hula* make pilgrimages to a temple set on the rocky Na Pali coast of Kauai. There they offer flower *lei* to Laka, the goddess of the hula.

On the edge of Halemaumau, the steaming sulfurous domain of the demigoddess Pele at Kilauea on Hawaii, numerous offering are left by Her worshippers. Leaf-wrapped volcanic rocks, scarlet berries of the *ohelo* (a close relative of the cranberry), incense, and other offerings are place there or thrown into the crater. During recent eruptions, such as those that consumed part of the Royal Gardens subdivision on Hawaii, homeowners who had invoked Pele reported that their houses had been spared the wrath of Her molten rock.

There are those who say that the Hawaiians have forgotten their old ways of worship and magic, that they no longer pray to Kane for rain, that they no longer see Hina in the Full Moon or Pele in the dancing fountains of fire. There are those who say the magic of Hawaii is long dead, buried under 150 years of Western dominance, religious conversion, and tons of concrete. First-time visitors arriving at Honolulu International Airport are apt to believe such statements. The long ride from the airport to Waikiki passes junkyards, heavy industrial areas, and shabby warehouses. The beach itself glitters with carefully groomed, imported sand, all but swallowed up by multimillion dollar hotels.

But above Honolulu, in the Tantalus Heights, lies Keaiwe Heiau. Now a state park, this ancient healing temple is still visited by the sick who leave offerings among its stones. An inscription on a plaque there reads:

> *A temple with life-giving powers believed to be a center*
> *where the Hawaiian Kahuna Lapa'au or herb doctor*
> *practiced the art of healing. Herbs grown in nearby*
> *gardens were compounded and prescribed with prayer.*
> —Commission of Historical Sites

Twenty or thirty minutes away at Wahiawa, in the center of the island, are *pohaku* (stones) with healing powers.

Most Hawaiians today are of "conventional" religious backgrounds. The missionaries, who first arrived in 1820 found the peoples ripe for the new religion. The Mormons made tremendous inroads. Their Polynesian Cultural Center, located in Laie on the island of Oahu, is the single most-visited attraction in the state.

Still, the earlier ways of existence on these islands—reverence for the earth, the sea, the sky, the water, and the plants—lives on. In 1984, a botanist told me that she prays to Ku for protection while hiking in the mountains. Time-honored deities are thanked prior to collecting flowers and foliage to create lei. Fishermen still attach *ki* leaves to their boats before setting out.

Many persons of Hawaiian ancestry still grow *dracaena* and ki plants outside their homes for money and protection, respectively. When ground is broken for new construction a kahuna is often called to bless the area with salt, water, and a ki leaf. The importance of this last ritual is affirmed by numerous stories of the accidents and strange occurrences at building sites at which it *wasn't* performed—workmen are killed, the earth itself sinks, heavy pieces of earth-moving equipment are found turned on their sides in the morning.

The kahuna is probably the least-understood aspect of ancient Hawaii. Numerous books have been written about them. Most are contradictory and bear little resemblance to the truth. One recently published book seems to combine the reminiscences of a Pleasant Hawaiian Holidays tour, faulty research, and some psychic detective work.

The kahuna were and are the keepers of the secret. These men and women were experts in various fields. In today's world, a persona with a PhD in psychology is a type of kahuna, as is a master sculptor, a skilled weather forecaster, a miraculously successful healer, an engineer, and a well-trained psychic.

There were kahuna who specialized in love magic, in navigation, in divination, in the construction of canoes and housing, in prayer. Far from the evil, scary creatures that the missionaries depicted them as, the kahuna were respected masters.

One of the best-known contemporary kahuna describes his field as philosophical, scientific, and magical practice. Kahuna aren't merely magicians. Several recent books have described *huna* as a purely psychological system. These are based on the works of Max Freedom Long, a researcher who, through investigating the Hawaiian language, sought to crack what he considered to be the "huna code." Unfortunately, Long never spoke to a kahuna, though they were around. His books—and those based on them—are sadly incomplete.

What is the heart of old Hawaii? It must lie in her people's views of deity. All their rites of worship, their temples, their magical practices stem from this people's relationships with the forces of nature.

Their deities, the personifications of the wind, the earth, volcanic activity, the fish, birds, and all the other features of their string of islands, were conceived of as being *real*, as real as those of any other religion and perhaps more so, since the earthly forms of their deities were all around them. No aspect of life was without religious impact. Fishermen prayed to Ku'ula for good catches; medicinal plants were gathered with prayers to Hina and Ku; all planting, harvesting, and eating were accompanied by prayers. Births and deaths, house building, sports of all kinds, even combat—all were overseen and nourished by the deities.

No one deity was revered above all others by all people at all times. Just as in ancient Egypt, certain gods and goddesses rose and fell in favor. Small geographic areas worshipped deities unknown to outsiders. The Hawaiians themselves describe, in the prayers that have been preserved, the 4,000, the 40,000, and 400,000 gods.

Pele is perhaps the most famous of them to outsiders, and yet, she wasn't quite a goddess. The woman of flame, who lives in Kiluaea on the island of Hawaii, is the *kupua*, or demi-goddess, who created the islands themselves through volcanic activity. Searching for a home for herself and her brothers and sisters, Pele dug pits for her fire that were free of groundwater. In turn, she created the islands from Ni'ihau to the Big Island of Hawaii, where she continues to live. On Kauai, two caves near Haena can still be seen. They represent earlier attempts of Pele's search to find a home.

Pele has not been forgotten by the Hawaiian people. As mentioned above, she is still given many offerings, and stories of her appearing in fire, steam, and mist during eruptions are commonplace. She is also said to show herself as a beautiful young girl or an old, wrinkled woman. Many drivers have reported picking up a female who stood by the side of the road. Within moments, she disappears from the car seat. That is Pele.

Though Pele is the spirit of the volcanoes, she isn't a wrathful being. Many see her as a true mother goddess, who continues to create new land when lava reaches the sea, stretching the size of the island of Hawaii. And unlike volcanic eruptions in most other parts of the world, those in Hawaii threaten little danger to human life.

———

There are many other Hawaiian deities:

Kane is seen in sunlight, fresh water, living creatures, and forests. Some myths credit him with creating the universe. Earthly forms of Kane include *ko* (sugar cane) as well as the beautiful *ohia lehua*, a tree bearing feathery red flowers.

Lono is the god of agriculture, fertility, the winds, gushing springs, and rain. He presides over many sports. At his *heiau*, people prayed for rain and rich crops, and offered plants and pigs to him. All Hawaiians ate from his food gourd. He is seen in the *kukui* tree, whose nuts were once made into lamps and are now fashioned into durable lei. Lono's other early forms include the *'ualu* (sweet potato) and the leaves of the *kalo*. From the root of the kalo (Tahitian: *taro*) poi is made.

Ku is the famous war-god of the ancient Hawaiians, the male generative power. It was at his temples that human sacrifices were made. *Kuka 'ilimoku*, one of the many forms of Ku, was made famous by Kamehamha I. A huge wooden statue of Kuka'ilimoku can be seen in the Bishop Museum in Honolulu. Other aspects of Ku (all the deities had many) include *Ku'ula*, the fisherman's god. Earthly forms of Ku include the hawk.

Human sacrifice has to be mentioned in any account of the ancient Hawaiians. It is certainly savage to our eyes, but it played an important ceremonial role at certain times. There has been speculation that the practice was introduced to Hawaii from outside its islands. (Before shaking our heads in horror, let's remember our own form of human sacrifice, one carried out on prisoners who are given death sentences. How different are we from the ancient Hawaiians?)

Hina is seen in the setting sun as well as in the moon. She rules over corals, spiny sea creatures, seaweeds, and cool forests. Women who beat tree bark into the cloth known as *kapa* (*tapa* elsewhere in the Pacific) prayed to Hina.

It may be surprising that **Poliahu** was revered by early Hawaiians, for she is a goddess of snow. However, Mouna Kea, on of the great volcanoes that make up the Big Island of Hawaii, is often shrouded with snow. It is the home of Poliahu, the beautiful goddess.

Laka oversaw the hula, which was originally both a sacred dance performed for the deities and the *ali'i* (chiefs) as well as a secular activity for the common people. Laka is represented on the hula altars by a block of wood wrapped with kappa cloth. Several plants, especially ferns, are sacred to her.

There are many other deities and demigods, such as Maui, the Hawaiian trickster who, among other exploits, fished up the islands from the bottom of the sea with his fishhook. Maui's magical hook can still be seen hanging in the skies over Hawaii, made up of stars. **Kamapua'a,** a demigod who appeared in various forms including that of a pig, had a tempestuous love affair with Pele. The mythology (sacred literature) of Hawaii is filled with passion, adventure, love, and magic. It is required reading for anyone wishing to pierce into ancient Hawaiian consciousness.

As we've seen, the ways of the past still live in Hawaii. It was recently proposed to tap a stream from Kilauea Crater in order to produce geothermal energy. Modern-day priestesses of Pele immediately protested, stating that she still lives in all parts of the crater and that the plan would be nothing more than selling part of her body. To their great dissatisfaction, the priestesses lost and the plans proceeded. Money overcame the old ways, as it often has.

Is there still magic to be found in Hawaii? Yes. It's there in the ground. In the air. In the cries of birds. In the rustling of plants. In the splash of water tumbling down a volcanic cliff. In the sunrise from Halakala. In the green, white, and black sand beaches. In the thundering waves.

Mana—the Hawaiian concept of the natural energy that resides in all things—permeates the very rock upon which these islands formed. The life-force is so vibrant here that the sensitive can feel it on the breeze when stepping off a 747 at the airport.

Yes, the magic of Hawaii lives in its people and the land itself. It is there, waiting, ready to reveal its secrets to anyone who goes with an open heart and open mind.

And it is alive!

Recommended Reading

Beckwith, Martha. *Hawaiian Mythology*. Honolulu: University Press of Hawaii. 1979.

Cox, J. Halley, and Edward Stasack. *Hawaiian Petroglyphs*. Honolulu: Bishop Museum Press, 1970.

Malo, David. *Hawaiian Antiquities*. Honolulu: Bishop Museum Press, 1971.

McDonald, Marie. *Ka Lei: The Leis of Hawaii*. Honolulu: Topgallant/Press Pacifica, 1985.

Mitchell, Donald D. Kilolani. *Resource Units in Hawaiian Culture*. Honolulu: The Kamehameha Schools Press/ Bernice P. Bishop Estate, 1982.

Stone, Margaret. *Supernatural Hawaii*. Honolulu: Aloha Graphics and Sales, 1979.

Ancient Greek Oracles

◇◇◇◇◇◇◇◇◇◇

Though there were three great oracles in ancient Greece—Trophonius, Dodona, and Delphi—it is the latter of these which is best remembered today.

The heart of these sacred places of prediction was the Pythia, the priestess who made the mystic pronouncements.

In the earliest times, the Pythia was chosen according to her youth, beauty, and noble background. Once a Pythia had been seduced and swept away by a handsome Thessalian, however, some changes were put into effect.

Thereafter, the Pythia was a woman of about fifty years of age from an obscure family background. Because of her ignoble birth, she was usually uneducated. However young or old she might be, the Pythia remained celibate for the length of her duties.

Before making oracular statements at Delphi, the Pythia was purified in a stream, robed, and crowned with laurel leaves (bay). Her priests escorted her into the Adyton, the underground chamber of the oracle at Delphi. There she was seated on a tripod beside a river that flowed through the subterranean chamber.

She probably inhaled the sulfurous fumes rising from cracks in the cavern's floor and further prepared herself by chewing bay leaves (thought to have a hallucinogenic effect). Bay leaves were also fumed in the cave.

Outside the Adyton, the client who came to seek knowledge made offerings of ritual cakes, gold treasures, and artwork (which supported the temple), and sacrificed a sheep or goat on the hearth. Once this had been done, he was escorted by the temple's priests into the sanctuary—far removed from the Pythia so that their presence didn't disturb her.

The question was put to the Pythia. She then entered an ecstatic state: chest heaving, eyes flashing, she tore her hair and violently trembled. Then, finally, she uttered a few words, which were duly recorded by her attendant priests.

These priests were of the utmost importance, for the Pythia's prophecies were usually couched in such obscure terms that an interpretation was necessary. Once the priest had written down the prophecy and handed it to the inquirer, the process was complete.

For over a thousand years, the Oracle at Delphi fulfilled the needs of tens of thousands of persons eager for a glimpse into the future. In its earliest days, the Pythia appeared no more than once a year. Kings and the wealthy upper class had to wait for this annual event, held on the seventh day of Bysios (roughly corresponding to our February-March).

Soon, however, demand grew so great that the oracles were opened once a month. Two or even three Pythia would be stationed at each shrine, and still the crush of need would overwhelm them.

Though only the richest could consult these mystic women, mass oracles were also held each year. According to old records, the Pythia simply sat on the steps leading to the temple and, in broad daylight, answered questions proffered by the populace.

Curiously, women (save for the Pythia) weren't allowed within the temple to consult the oracle. They were forced to send male friends to ask.

Not surprisingly, the bulk of the prophecies proved themselves to be true, though the inquirer often misinterpreted the priest's translations.

The philosopher Cicero, who was a famous skeptic, stated, "Never could the oracle of Delphi have been so overwhelmed with so many important offerings from monarchs and nations if all the ages had not proved the truth of its oracles."

Though Delphi was justifiably famous, the other two oracles were more obscure. That at Dodona consisted of a shrine near a sacred oak forest. The Pythia simply went to the prophetic oak on a riverbank, stood beneath it, and listened to the sound of the moving leaves or the stream (which sprang from a nearby spring). Each sound possessed a separate, distinct meaning (recorded in a book), which led to the inquirer's answer.

The third oracle, known as Trophonius after the architect of that at Delphi, was physically similar to its more famous sister, but consulting it was a terrifying experience. At night, the querent climbed down a ladder, wriggled feet-first through a long, narrow tunnel, and then sat on some type of device that swiftly carried him deeper and deeper into the earth.

Throughout this demanding process, he was forced to carry a honey cake in each hand—failure to do so resulted in death. If he survived this, he was allowed to hear the Pythia's words.

The oracles of ancient Greece were important social and political centers, and the phenomenon of world leaders consulting psychics hasn't yet ended.

Zeus Help Us

◇◇◇◇◇◇◇◇◇◇

Sneezing has long been one of the most mysterious of our in-voluntary actions. The fact that sneezes usually occur without warning, and can rarely be stifled, led to their use as an oracle of the future.

From the classical period to the Middle Ages, sneezes were considered omens. To sneeze to the left (i.e., to feel it emanating from that side) was a sign of misfortune. To the right, a positive omen. To sneeze early in the day was favorable; to do so later or at night, unfavorable.

Additionally, a sneeze could also be an automatic exorcism, marking the withdrawal of an evil spirit, who might then wreak havoc on others near the sneezer. To halt any such problems, Greeks said "Zeus help us!" when one of their number sneezed.

Sneezing provokes the giving of similar good wishes in all parts of the world. These often call upon deities or health to avert the possible danger. Germans may say "Gesundheit" ("Health!"). Some English-speaking peoples invoke their concept of God to *"bless"* the sneezer, while the ancient Hawaiians stated *"Kihe, a Mauliola."* ("Sneeze, and may you have a long life.") Connections between sneezing and deity are common and ancient Aristotle wrote that "We consider sneezing as something divine."

Among the fortunate days upon which to sneeze are New Year's Eve and New Year's Day. Sneezing then is believed to provide great fortune to the sneezer during the following year.

Hecate

◇◇◇◇◇◇◇◇◇◇

Hecate is perhaps the most famous of the Greek deities associated with magic. According to tradition, she was the daughter of Zeus and Demeter, or Perses and Asteria, or Zeus and Hera. Though her pedigree is unclear, it seems certain that Hecate was a Titan of Thracian origin.

From the earliest times she ruled the Moon, the Earth, and the sea. Among her blessings were wealth, victory, wisdom, and successful sailing and hunting, but she withheld these from those mortals who didn't deserve them.

She was the sole Titan who retained such powers under the iron rule of Zeus, and was honored by all the immortal deities. She even participated in the war with the Gigantes (giants). In time, her power grew so that she was associated with many other goddesses: as queen of nature, she was identified with Demeter, Rhea, and Cybele; as a huntress, protectress of youth, and moon goddess, with Artemis.

Later in Greek history, it was stated that Hecate was the sole deity (aside from Helios) who observed the abduction of Persephone. She left her cave and, torch in hand, assisted Demeter in her search.

Once Persephone had been found, Hecate remained with Persephone as her companion. This gave Hecate formidable powers over the underworld, and she became a goddess of purification and protection, accompanied by her dogs.

Hecate is best remembered today as a dark goddess, who at night sent out demons and phantoms; who taught magic and sorcery to brave mortals; who wandered with the souls of the dead after dark. Her approach was always heralded by the cries and howls of dogs. Despite this, she was also invoked for protection and was greatly loved.

Her home is alternately described as a cave, among tombs, near crossroads or within sight of a place where blood has been spilled during a murder. Images of Hecate are sometimes of a normal woman, but others represent her as possessing three heads.

Her worship was widespread, especially in Samothrace, Aegina, Argos, and in Athens, where she was honored in a sanctuary near the acropolis. In Athens, many homes displayed small statues of Hecate, which were either inside or outside the home. Such images were also placed at crossroads, and there is speculation that these Hecataea (images of Hecate) were consulted as oracles. At the end of each month, her worshipers set out dishes of food for her at a crossroads (where two roads crossed each other.) Honey and black female lambs were among her sacrifices. Hecate, then, is a complex goddess: giver of wealth and fortune, and mistress of sorcery. Even as late as the early 1600s, Shakespeare included Hecate in *Macbeth*, and she is still worshiped today by those unafraid of her awesome powers.

Birds of the Deities

◇◇◇◇◇◇◇◇◇◇

Birds have long been viewed as messengers of goddesses and gods. Their quickness, obvious intelligence, and often beautiful forms, coupled with their ability to fly, led to their intimate connection with deity throughout the world.

Birds in general have often been considered to be messengers of the deities. Many cultures linked them with the human soul, and the common English expression, "a little bird told me," stems from ancient beliefs that birds could communicate with humans and pass on important information.

A few of the birds that have been associated with deities are listed here:

Apollo (Greek god of the arts, healing, and light):
Raven, crow, hawk, swan

Athena (Greek goddess of wisdom, learning, and war):
Crow, owl

Brahma (Hindu creator god): Goose

Eros (Greek god of love): Goose

Hera (Greek goddess of childbirth, home, and marriage):
Crow, goose

Horus (Egyptian Sun god): Hawk, eagle

Ishtar (Babylonian goddess of love and fertility): Dove

Isis (Egyptian goddess of all things): Goose

Juno (Roman goddess of marriage, home, and childbirth):
Goose, peacock

Jupiter (Roman supreme deity): Eagle

Kami (Hindu god of love): Sparrow

Kane (Hawaiian god of fresh water, sunlight, winds,
and procreation): Owl

Ku (Hawaiian god of fishing, war, and sorcery): Hawk

Lilith (Mesopotamian goddess of night, evil, and death): Owl

Ma (Egyptian mother goddess): Vulture

Maat (Egyptian goddess of truth): Ostrich

Minerva (Roman goddess of wisdom): Owl

Nekhbet (Egyptian mother goddess; goddess of the underworld): Vulture

Osiris (Egyptian god of the dead, resurrection, and agriculture): Heron

Peitho (Greek goddess of winning speech): Goose

Priapus (Roman god of fertility): Goose

Ra (Egyptian Sun god): Hawk, goose

Thoth (Egyptian god of learning, writing): Ibis

The Valkyries (Norse goddesses who selected those who would die in battle): Raven

Venus (Roman goddess of love): Dove, goose, swallow

Yama (Hindu god of the dead): Owl, pigeon

Zeus (Supreme deity of ancient Greece): Eagle, swan, pigeon

Iris: Goddess
of the Rainbow

◇◇◇◇◇◇◇◇◇◇

The multicolored arcs that appear in the sky after or during a rain have long captured the imagination. Rainbows are, by their nature, intangible and fleeting things, possessed of magic and mystery. They've played an important role in shaping our mystic consciousnesses and have been closely associated with religion for thousands of years.

The most famous deity of the rainbow is Iris, the gentle great goddess of peace. Her name means either "the messenger" or "I join," both of which suggest that Iris is the conciliator or the messenger of the deities, who restores peace to nature (much as a rainbow usually indicates the end of a storm).

Iris was the daughter of Electra and sister to the Harpies. She was one of the divine messengers who carried news from Mount Ida to Mount Olympus from deities to deities, and from deities to humans. She was primarily engaged in service by Hera and Zeus, but even Achilles once asked her to help him call the winds. Iris didn't only respond to divine command, however, for she also offered assistance on her own initiative.

She was intimately connected with the rainbow. It was the only road on which she traveled. Thus it appeared at her command and vanished when no longer needed. In very early Greek religion, the rainbow was seen as the "swift messenger" of the deities, even before it became particularly associated with Iris.

No statues of Iris have been preserved. Still, frequent representations of her on vases—and in bas-relief reveal her form.

She's often shown as a beautiful woman, usually dressed in a long, wide tunic covered with a lighter garment. A pair of wings sprouts from her shoulders, and she carries a herald's staff in her left hand. A rainbow arches above her.

Some representations depict her as flying, with wings outstretched from both her shoulders and her sandals. While flying she carries the staff as well as a pitcher.

———

Little is known about her worship today. It seems to have been centered on the Island of Delos, where her worshipers offered her cakes made from wheat, honey, and dried figs.

The Delians apparently greatly appreciated the help of Iris. Upon one occasion, Leto, who was in labor on Delos, was delayed nine days from giving birth (to Apollo and Artemis) by Hera. The Delians promised Iris a necklace of gold and electron nine cubits long if she would come to Delos to assist with the birth. She did, and all went well.

Though little is known about Iris today, her symbol still shines in the skies above Greece after storms, and she may yet walk the multicolored stairway to Mount Olympus, to report on the activities that occur far below.

> *Whatso'er thy heart desire*
> *Write it well in words of fire.*
> *Cut the sacred apple through*
> *Place the wish between the two.*
>
> *Seal with twigs of lady's tree*
> *Place in kiln till dried it be.*
> *Sleep upon it night or day*
> *Till good fortune comes your way.*

Ancient Egyptian Incense

◇◇◇◇◇◇◇◇◇

Few other cultures have valued scent as greatly as did the ancient Egyptians. They rubbed their bodies and hair with scented oils, bathed in perfumed water, inhaled the aromas of flowers during banquets, and placed cones of scented wax on their heads so that the aroma would be released as the wax melted down onto their wigs. Even food was perfumed, and banquets frequently took place in rooms strewn with rose petals.

Incense was also widely used in Egyptian religion and magic. The most famous of Egyptian incense materials, frankincense, was but one of the both delightful and strange ingredients burned in vessels of fire.

Many ancient Egyptian incenses can't be made today, for some contain unidentifiable ingredients. Still, a few clear formulae have been preserved.

An all-purpose divinatory incense was made from frankincense, wax, storax, turpentine, and datestones. These were ground together with wine, formed into a ball, and placed on the fire.

To make spirits quickly gather to answer questions during divination, burn stalks of the herb anise and crocodile egg shells.

Other simple formulae include: crocodile bile and myrrh, burned to "bring the gods in by force" and crocus and alum, which were censed to "bring in a thief."

Ancient Egyptian
Spell to Cure a Dog Bite

◇◇◇◇◇◇◇◇◇◇

Little is known today of folk magic in ancient Egypt. Though we have records of state rituals, not much was recorded regarding the simple magic of the common people.

One of the few sources of such workings is contained in what is today known as the Leiden Papyrus. This papyrus was collected in Thebes in the early 1800s and was probably written about 300 CE. Though it is of a late date, it bears little Greek and/or Christian influence.

The unnamed scribe who created this 16-foot papyrus didn't write the rituals; he simply copied them from other papyri. Thus, it seems clear that much of the information dates from 100 to 200 years earlier than its compilation, still within the Greek period of Egypt but closer to the purer Egyptian culture.

The papyrus is a motley collection of spells. Several sections outline methods of divination, usually involving a "pure boy" (who is ritually prepared to see the spirits). Other sections include erotic recipes, cures for a variety of ailments, a few spells "to create madness" and the like. One of these spells runs thus:

Spell Spoken
To the Bite of the Dog

"I have come forth from Arkhah, my mouth being full of blood of a black dog. I spit it out, the ... of a dog. O this dog, who is among the ten dogs which belong to Anubis, the son of his body, extract your venom, remove your saliva from me again. If you do not extract your venom and remove your saliva, I will take you up to the court of the temple of Osiris, my watchtower. I will do for you the parapage of birds, like the voice of Isis, the sorceress, the mistress of sorcery, who bewitches everything and is not bewitched in her name of Isis the sorceress."

And you pound garlic with kmou [unidentified plant] and you put it on the wound of the bite of the dog, and you address it daily until it is well.

An Old Divination

◇◇◇◇◇◇◇◇◇◇

Humans have invented many ingenious methods of peering into the future. Coffee grounds and crystal spheres, tarot cards and pendulums, observation of the movements of animals, the shapes of clouds, and the ripples of water are but a few of these techniques.

A lesser-known divination, of uncertain heritage, requires simple tools: a sieve (or colander), seven small bivalve (clam) shells, one black bean, and one white bean.

To use the oracle, place all items into the sieve. Shake it seven times, from the left to the right. Stop and look for these things:

- The position of the shells relative to the beans

- The number of shells that have landed upright
  (i.e., with the dome-shaped surface facing up)
  or upside down (the hollow portion facing up)

Here are some of the prophecies that can be seen:

- 4 to 7 shells, hollow side up, near the white bean:
  luck, success, long life, fulfilling relationship

- 4 to 7 shells, dome side up, near the white bean:
  accident or illness

- 4 to 7 shells, hollow side up, near the black bean:
  a period of luck interrupted by tribulations

- 4 to 7 shells, dome side up, near the black bean:
  problems with money or business

- 4 shells, hollow side up, forming a circle near the
  white bean: a legacy; a windfall

- 4 shells, hollow side up, forming a circle near the
  black bean: sadness

- 3 shells, dome side up, forming a triangle near
  the white bean: wishes will *come* to fruition

- 3 shells, hollow side up, forming a triangle near
  the black bean: concentrate on the present

- Any number of shells, either side up, forming a
  cross near the white bean: sadness

- Any number of shells, either side up, forming a crescent: luck and blessings

- All shells, dome side up: strength

- All shells, hollow side up: love and peace

Note: All such tools of divination can be effective only if they contact the psychic mind. Otherwise, they're but toys. If this form doesn't speak to you, search for another. Many have found their perfect divinatory tool in the tarot, others in the pendulum, rune stones, and the I Ching.

The tool isn't as important as the effect that it has upon you, so carefully choose it.

The Man in the Moon

◇◇◇◇◇◇◇◇◇◇

On the night of the Full Moon when the shimmering globe rises slowly from the eastern horizon, look into its face. The dark areas of the Moon's surface contain an image. What is this figure?

Persons in China, Japan, Tibet, India, Mexico, Eastern Europe, and elsewhere see a rabbit. Many stories are still told of how a rabbit hopped to the Moon and took up residence on its cold surface.

In Hawaii and throughout Polynesia, the Moon is thought to be inhabited not by a rabbit (an unknown creature), but by a Goddess, Hina. In Hawaii, Hinaikamala (Hina of the Moon) had grown tired of constantly making bark cloth, so she took her *ipu* (gourd container) and climbed "by the rainbow path" up to the Sun. Finding her new home to be too hot, she went instead to the Moon and can still be seen on its face with her gourd by her side.

The Moon is usually linked with lunar animals (such as rabbits and hares) and with women or goddesses (Hina). Thus, when children today gaze up, trying to see the "man in the Moon" they're often disappointed, for no "man" is visible.

Memories of the hare or woman in the Moon may have been forgotten as the new faith overwhelmed earlier Western pagan religions. Seeing a woman or hare in the Moon wasn't favored by those of the new religion, due to their connections with Moon-worship and totemism.

What to do? The story of the "man in the Moon" was invented and neatly filled the bill.

But elsewhere, far removed from the effects of this new religion, a rabbit with floppy ears and tail or a woman sitting beside her gourd, are still seen on clear evenings on the Moon's glowing face.

The man in the Moon isn't.

Moon Spells

Upon seeing the Full Moon, form a circle with the thumb and first finger of your talented hand. Hold it up until the Moon rests within this ring, and say these words in a hushed voice:

Good moon, round moon,
Full moon near:
Let the future
Now appear.

Gaze at the Moon and ask a question; it shall be answered.

Under the dim light of the waning Moon, write on a piece of paper that from which you wish to be freed. Tear the paper in half three times and bury it. Then say:

Pray to the moon when she be slivered
From ill you shall be delivered.
All that has harmed me now is bound:
Down, down beneath the ground.

———

Take a piece of silver (jewelry or a coin), a cup, and a pitcher of water out under the light of the Moon. Pour the water into the cup. Place the silver into the cup. Stir the water thrice clockwise with a finger. Holding the cup, walk thrice in a clockwise circle beneath the Moon while saying these words:

O moon light
Wrap me tight
Guard me now
Day and night.

Drink the water, then retrieve the coin or jewelry. Wear or carry the silver for one lunar month for protection. Repeat if needed on the next Full Moon.

To create prophetic dreams, walk outside with a fresh white rose. Hold it up to the Moon between both hands so that the blossom is flooded with Moonlight. Say:

Awaken my second sight

Press the white rose against your forehead, saying:

By the power of this rite

Place the flower under your pillow before sleep and remember your dreams.

———

Scrape the rind from a ripe lemon. Allow to dry for seven nights on a ceramic plate. On the seventh night, take the plate, a small square piece of white cloth, and a threaded needle outside. By the light of the Moon, transfer the dried lemon peel to the center of the cloth. Fold the cloth in half, creating a triangle. Quickly stitch together the two open sides with the threaded needle. When you've finished your work, hold it up to the Moon and say:

The charm is made!

Place it under your pillow for restful sleep at night.

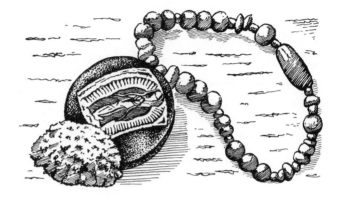

Mexican Magic

◇◇◇◇◇◇◇◇◇◇◇

Contemporary Mexican folk magic is the result of a complex mixing of cultures bearing clear signs of Aztec, Roman Catholic, European, and even Buddhist influences.

In nearly every town in this predominantly Catholic country, charms can be secured from herbalists, street vendors, and at open-air markets. Since charms are concrete representatives of underlying beliefs, we'll first examine a few of these.

The *Piedra iman* (lodestone) is a common magical tool. Unlike those sold in the United States, they're rarely painted but are usually covered with clinging iron filings. Such natural magnets are carried, worn, or hung in homes and businesses to attract love or for protective purposes. In some villages, they're washed every Tuesday and Friday with wine.

Piedra iman are sometimes packed with wheat and sewn into red cloth. On this cloth is a picture of San Martin de Caballero (Saint Martin the Horseman). Such charms are made to guard against hunger and to instill protection. (A Mexican magician also taught me to place a Piedra iman in a triangle for positive vibrations.)

The *Ojo de Venado* ("deer's eye") is a charm given to children for protection. It consists of a large, flat, nut-brown seed with a circular band of black. A red string is usually threaded through the seed. Attached to the thread may be a tassel of red thread, beads, or a small section of a magical wood.

A household charm is known as *Coronita Ajo*. This is a small wreath made of separate cloves of garlic strung onto a wire and entwined with red ribbon. It is hung in the home (or business) for good luck and to guard against evil.

Perhaps the most famous—and grisly—of all Mexican charms is the *chuparosa* (hummingbird). This consists of a small, dried hummingbird wrapped with red cloth. This relic is used in love-attracting rituals.

Yet another protective charm is known as the *herradura* (horseshoe). These are small horseshoe-shaped magnets wrapped in red ribbon, packaged in cellophane along with a saint's picture and small packets of herbs. At times, a small representation of Buddha may also be included with the herradura. These charms are used in businesses to drive away evil and to invite prosperity and customers.

Siete Machos is the name of a cologne manufactured in Mexico. Its strong scent has led to its use in numerous healing and anti-bewitchment rites. (The bottle's label shows smoke rising from a censer, surrounded by seven goat's heads.)

Other uses include mixing Siete Machos with Florida water (a cologne). This is splashed on the body every fifteen days for internal purification.

These few examples clearly show the multicultural nature of many contemporary Mexican charms. The hummingbird was sacred to the ancient Aztecs. The saints are often seen as Catholic versions of pre-Christian deities, and are utilized in decidedly non-Christian ways.

Garlic was imported from Europe by the conquistadors. Images of the Buddha, which are frequent in charms, could only have been late introductions.

Mexican folk spells are far more difficult to uncover, for such actions are secret and are usually performed in privacy. Here are a few, and they differ little from those of Europe. All of these involve love.

For marriage, a handful of basil is impregnated with the magician's favorite perfume or cologne. This mixture is then buried in a flowerpot.

A love perfume is created by collecting seven roses on a Friday after sunset. The petals of these roses are mixed with one liter of water and seven drops of the practitioner's favorite perfume or cologne. The magician is directed to bathe normally that evening but to rinse with the mixture. This rite is repeated for seven consecutive Fridays.

It must be noted that the use of such charms and spells usually isn't regarded as magic (which is universally believed to involve devil-worship, another Spanish influence), but as religion. The predominance of the saints in many magical charms suggests that many of these persons are performing religious magic in a broadly Catholic way.

Four-Leaf Clover

◇◇◇◇◇◇◇◇◇◇

Many tales are told today concerning our sixteenth president. It is widely known that, during his lifetime, Lincoln was interested in spiritualism, astrology, and other arcane matters. He is said to have even held seances in the White House. What is little known, however, was his apparent belief in the powers of a well-known herbal charm: the four-leaf clover.

Four-leaf clovers are popular magical talismans carried for a variety of purposes: to draw luck generally; to attract money, health and wisdom; to promote love. Among the more sinister of the traditional powers of four-leaf clovers is that its bearer is able to detect the presence of evil spirits.

Precisely why Lincoln carried a four-leaf clover (if he did; this is still subject to debate) is unclear at this late date, but his alleged charm did manage to create more recent history.

In the 1920s, international tennis champion William T. Tilden II was about to face Gerald Patterson at Wimbledon. The day before the first match, a friend presented Tilden with Lincoln's clover for luck. He soon defeated Patterson and, in fact, won every match until the magic sprig was misplaced. Fortunately, the clover reappeared just before he won back the American tennis title in 1929.

The "king of nets" placed great faith in this little relic of a past era. Lincoln's thoughts regarding this four-leaf clover are unknown, but it's refreshing to know that at least one American president may have relied upon the powers of herb magic.

It seems clear that Lincoln didn't have his four-leaf clover with him when he went to Ford's Theatre on April 15, 1865—the day of his assassination.

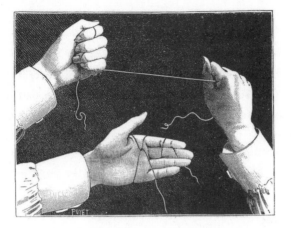

The Magic of String

◇◇◇◇◇◇◇◇◇◇

When I was very young, my family sponsored an exchange student from Iran. After telling me exotic stories of his homeland (our countries were then on friendly terms), the young man taught me how to make several string figures that he'd learned as a boy.

Stunned at the prospects of creating intricate patterns with something as simple as a piece of string, I soon grilled my friends and learned how to create a few other string figures. One of the mysteries that I learned was that, if two persons correctly played cat's cradle for a very long time, the strings would automatically make a rare and unusual pattern. I could never play long enough to discover if this was true.

Even at the age of ten, I was a researcher, and soon read a book on the subject. I became fascinated by string figures.

Little did I know that persons around the world had created similar figures; that many of them were made for religious or magical purposes, and that in most cultures everyone, from the youngest children to the elders, made string figures.

Among the areas where string figures were made are Alaska, Canada, the continental United States (the Apache, Tewa, Zuni, Pawnee, Navajo, Omaha, and Cherokee are among the peoples who made them), Peru, Paraguay, Hawaii, Guyana, Angola, Botswana, and South Africa.

The Philippines, Australia, New Zealand, Melanesia, Fiji, the Society Islands (including Tahiti), Tikopia, New Caledonia, the Gilbert Islands, Japan, Korea, China, Denmark, Germany, Austria, Switzerland, France, and the Netherlands were other places where string figures were made.

Ethnologists began recording string figures and their methods of construction in the late 1800s. Unfortunately, they often failed to similarly record the mythic or magical history that accompanied the creation of these figures, so our information is limited.

On the Gilbert Islands (in Melanesia), Ububwe was the god of the string figures. After death, the human soul was carefully questioned by Ububwe regarding its knowledge of string figures before it was allowed to enter the underworld.

In Alaska, the string was seen to possess magical power when properly used. Ritual string figures were made during winter to snare the Sun and prevent its departure. Additionally, boys of this area were forbidden to play cat's cradle, as this might result in their hands becoming entangled in the harpoon line later on in life.

In many lands, string figures were made to represent deities. Certain words chanted over the figure reinforced its association with the deity, and creating the string figures may well have been a form of ritual invocation.

So magic can be found in the most curious of places, even in the games that many of us learned in our youth. Much has been lost, but the most famous form, cat's cradle, is known in Germany to this day as *hexenspiel*: witch's game.

Cat's Eye

There is an old saying that if you fear nightly intrusion by ghosts or evil spirits, you should hang a piece of knotted string from your door handle before you lie down to sleep.

Your unwanted visitor will have to untie every single knot before it may enter the room—and with any luck the sun will be up by then!

Magic Wells

◇◇◇◇◇◇◇◇◇◇

Throughout the world, water has been rightly regarded as a sustainer of life. From this observation it was but a small step to acknowledge bodies of water fresh and salt—as the dwelling places of spirits and deities.

Rivers (such as the Ganges, the Nile, and the Euphrates) have long been worshiped as manifestations of deity. In England, the river Severn was the goddess Sabrina, to whom flower offerings were thrown at regular intervals.

Many peoples of North America similarly made offerings of beads and tobacco to river spirits. Such rites honoring water spirits are also known from Africa, Sri Lanka, Korea, Mexico, France, Germany, and throughout Europe.

The oceans have long been honored in the persons of Tiamat, Kanaloa, Poseidon, Llyr, and Neptune, among other deities. But wells, both natural (springs) or artificially created, have garnered more than their share of worship and magical observances in Britain and Europe.

The charming custom of well-dressing still continues in some parts of Britain. This ancient practice, in which specific wells are decorated with flowers, is now associated with various saints and is conducted with due religious ceremony. However, it stems from the most antique days, long before the introduction of Christianity.

As early as the sixth century CE, Gildas wrote of Britons paying homage to wells and rivers. From the sixth to the twelfth century, various English kings and religious leaders passed laws forbidding well-worship. Fortunately, their efforts were in vain, and over 100 wells are recorded as having received honors.

With the growing acceptance of Christianity throughout Britain, the conversion of the wells began. Those that had once been sacred to Celtic or Teutonic goddesses were transferred to the saints or even to Mary herself.

But the magic continued. Many wells possessed healing waters, and some, such as that at Buxton, became quite famous. Even Queen Mary visited this well on numerous occasions, and wrote of the "incredible" nature of the water's cure. By this time, the well had been rededicated to St. Anne.

There were many types of magic wells in Wales, Scotland, and Ireland: holy wells, rag wells, wishing wells, pin wells, and even cursing wells.

Holy wells were those associated with goddesses, such as the famous Chalice Well at Glastonbury. Virtually all wells were once considered to be "holy," as water is a divine substance.

Rag wells are places of healing where the supplicants tied small bits of cloth onto nearby bushes and trees as an offering to the spirit or deity of the well.

Wishing wells are quite familiar. A coin was thrown into the well with a "wish." The wisher then noted the number of bubbles that arose and their size and, from these signs, determined whether the wish would be granted. (The object tossed into the well constituted payment to the well's spirit.)

Pin wells were similar. Pins (or buttons) were tossed into the well, and once again their movements indicated whether the wisher would be granted her or his wish. Additionally, bent pins were thrown into such wells for luck and as a protection against evil magic.

Cursing wells were much rarer. These were usually lonely places where it was believed that the well's attendant spirit or deity would send curses to one's enemies. Oval or circular stones were sometimes turned before such wells, and the curser walked widdershins (counterclockwise) around the well.

The rarest of all are the laughing wells. The waters of such springs usually possess natural carbonation, so that when small, heavy objects are thrown into them, a frenzy of bubbles is released. Little magical information regarding them has been recorded.

At all but the cursing wells, the supplicant walked thrice clockwise around the well before praying or wishing; only then was the water drunk or the offering made.

Many spells have been created using well water, but most have been curative. Pliny (AD 77) writes: "Mix water in equal proportions from three different wells, and, after making a libation with parts of it in a new earthen vessel, administer the rest to patients suffering from fever." The water from three wells would understandably be considered to be even more potent than that collected from just one source.

Divinations were also made with well water. In Scotland, the water from St. Andrew's Well was poured in a wooden bowl and placed beside a patient. A small ceramic dish was gently laid on the surface of the water. If, while floating, it slowly rotated clockwise, the patient would recover. If counterclockwise, no recovery was in sight.

Many wells, lakes, fountains, and decorative pools to this day are littered with coins tossed by those who may well be unaware of the pagan origins of such practices.

The Magic
of Scott
Cunningham

By Donald Michael Kraig

Acknowledgments

I would like to gratefully thank Marilee Bigelow for her friendship and editorial comments. Marilee was one of Scott's best friends, often sharing her recipes with him as well as accompanying him on several adventures to Hawaii. I have no doubt that her friendship helped Scott become a better person. I know her friendship has done that for me.

Enormous thanks also go to Holly Allender Kraig for her excellent editorial suggestions.

Another thanks goes to Bill Krause for his guidance and for backing this project. His positive attitude about my work was responsible for this book. I am very pleased with the result, and it's due to Bill's encouragement.

And finally, I have to acknowledge Scott Cunningham. His life touched so many of us, his magic changed the world, and his friendship changed my life forever.

Introduction: Scott and Me

It began with rain.

I had been living north of San Diego in the beach town of Encinitas on a street called Vulcan. One morning I was awakened early. The landlord decided to resurface the flat roof by hiring some locals to replace the roof's tarpaper and gravel. It was a noisy, messy activity, and they didn't clean up afterward. They also didn't do a good job because a week later, during the season's first heavy rain (yes, it does rain in California), the roof turned into a sieve. I put pots and pans everywhere but couldn't keep up with the intruding rainwater. The squishy carpet became moldy and the sickly sweet air became difficult to breathe. I had to find a place to move... fast!

There was a store in San Diego called Ye Olde Enchantment Shoppe where I had been giving workshops on magic, Tarot, Kabalah, Tantra, etc. I went in and asked the owner, Judith Wise (who is now, sadly, in the Summerland), if she knew anyone with a place to rent. She told me that there was a young man looking for a roommate. He was an author. I went to his apartment, measured the room that was available, figured that it would work for me, and shook his hand. I moved in on February 29, 1980, the extra day of that leap year. Thus began six years of sharing an apartment with Scott Cunningham.

Although Scott was born in Michigan (in 1956), his family moved to San Diego in 1959 where, excluding brief trips, he lived for the rest of his life. He told me that he had always felt different, but it wasn't until high school that he saw his future.

From a young age, Scott had been interested in nature and in herbs. In 1971, his mother gave him a copy of *The Supernatural* by Hill and Williams. The book included Italian folk hand signs used to do such things as give protection and repel the "evil eye." A few years later, a girl in his high school, whom I'll call "D," recognized the signs and introduced herself. They became friends, and she introduced him to more magic and to Witchcraft. From this time on, natural magic, Witchcraft, and writing became the focus of the rest of his life.

Scott joined the Navy, but the extreme regimentation didn't agree with his nature. He performed some magic and achieved the result he desired: an early yet honorable discharge.

Scott took a number of odd jobs, ranging from working at a Jack in the Box fast food "restaurant" to a typist at the Scripps Institute of Oceanography. He went on to college, studying creative writing. He dropped out after two years because he had more published articles and books than most of his professors. To earn a living, Scott became what I like to call a "hack writer." To outsiders, hacks are usually thought of as bad writers, but the truth is they do something that is very challenging. They are paid to write articles or books on a specific topic. Even if they're unfamiliar with the topic, they have to learn all they can and write an article or book that indicates they know everything. Few people can do this believably and well, but Scott was able to do so. For example, while we shared that apartment he wrote articles for truck and automobile magazines although he had little personal interest in the subject.

One of the things I admired about Scott was his incredible focus. When he was working on a book almost nothing could get in his way ... except the need for money. Many times, toward the end of the month, I'd knock on his door and remind him that his truck columns would be due soon. I did that because he'd get paid quickly and together we could pay the rent. He'd stop typing and leave without saying a thing. But I knew what was going on. He was going to the library to do research for his next column. I like to think that my reminders helped us to stay in that apartment.

At the time I moved in, Scott was already publishing novels, and his first nonfiction book, *Magical Herbalism*, had been accepted for publication. During those pre-computer days, Scott was using one of the finest typewriters available—a red IBM Selectric. Although the output was beautiful, there were so many moving parts in it that it would frequently break down. He had a contract with a repair company to come out and fix it when needed. I still remember hearing him tapping keys as the words flew out of him at a tremendous rate, followed by selective tapping (when he realized that something was wrong), and then the pounding of his fists on the table as he yelled, "Damn! Damn! Damn!" A phone call to the repair company ensued.

That cursing showed he had a temper, which was clearly evidenced when his eyes flashed in a certain way. However, it was never directed toward me. I still find it amazing that although the apartment was small, we never had a real argument. I think it was because we respected each other, gave each other plenty of room, and used each other as "sounding boards" to share ideas.

Among the many things I admired about Scott, there was one thing that was truly outstanding. In all of his occult writings he would only include spells, formulas, and lore under two conditions: first, if it was from a historical source, and second, if he tested it out himself. He would never simply make things up and put them in his books.

For the next decade his occult writing focused on natural magic. His personal life was one of constant searching and yearning to know more of the Goddess, as well as have a closer relationship with Her. At this time Wicca, or Witchcraft (during those years the two words were synonymous) was primarily focused on the group structure known as a *coven*. You needed to be initiated into a coven to practice The Craft. He became involved with numerous groups, but inevitably became disenchanted with them for one reason or another. These experiences, combined with his personal research and mental logic led him to ask two questions:

- *Why do you have to be initiated to worship The Goddess?*

- *If Witchcraft is an initiatory religion, who initiated the first Witch?*

This resulted in Scott working a great deal on his own rather than in covens. Meanwhile, Scott's publisher, Llewellyn, had been doing well with a series called the Truth Abouts. These were small booklets on a single topic meant to sell for $1.95. They asked Scott to do one on Witchcraft. The booklet's popularity was such that they asked Scott to do a larger book on that subject. *The Truth About Witchcraft Today* (1988) became a huge hit, bringing the subject to tens of thousands of new people and making very clear that Scott Cunningham was more than a folk magician, he was a Witch.

But there were those two nagging questions! He came to the conclusion that you don't have to be initiated to worship

The Goddess or to be a Witch. The result was a book that revolutionized Wicca, Witchcraft, Paganism, and the world: *Wicca: A Guide for the Solitary Practitioner*. Without this book, many other books about solitary Witchcraft would have never been published, and hundreds of thousands of people would not be part of Wicca and Witchcraft today. Scott really did use the magic of the written word to change the world.

Scott continued to write novels (mostly using pseudonyms such as "Cathy Cunningham" or "Dirk Fletcher") as well as books on natural magic and Wicca and Witchcraft. He became involved with some people who had a group that practiced in Hawaii. Scott began to visit them, and his natural fascination for research led him to the study of local natural magic found in Hawaiian history, legends, and lore. For the rest of his life, Hawaii and its magic became a focus. Even when he was quite ill he would travel to Hawaii several times each year to do research. Scott visited numerous sacred sites, spent untold hours in Hawaiian libraries, and talked with both experts and locals. He was only able to write one book on the subject before his untimely passing.

In 1983, Scott was diagnosed with lymphoma. He had surgery, followed by chemotherapy. In the middle of the chemotherapy he had to change doctors and the new doctor restarted the chemotherapy, making this treatment last longer than usual. It was very challenging for Scott. He would come home from the treatment and have an hour to drink a gallon—sixteen cups—of water to flush his system.

During our time sharing the apartment there were periods when both Scott and I were short on funds. We never loaned or gave each other money, but we would do things like buy from the other some of the books we each owned. Some of these books went between us several times. We'd also buy each other dinner or pay for movies. Scott didn't like it when I would (rather loudly) comment on how something in a movie was incredibly stupid.

I eventually moved out when I was offered a good-paying job about a hundred miles away. Scott stayed in the apartment for several years before moving to a nicer place. We remained friends for the remainder of Scott's life. People always say, "We'll stay in touch," when they move apart, but distance does take its toll. We didn't see as much of each other as I would have liked.

Scott and I would make rude comments about each other as jokes. We never took the comments seriously because we knew they weren't true, we respected each other, and we knew that we each had a strong enough personality to withstand the jabs. We did this with others, too, but only if we respected them and knew they wouldn't be bothered by it.

I learned so much from Scott. Of course, I learned a great deal about Wicca and Witchcraft, Paganism, herbology, incense, and natural magic. He wasn't my teacher, nor was I his teacher when it came to topics of Kabalah and ceremonial magic. We'd just talk and share and learn from each other.

I also learned a lot about the craft of writing from Scott. This came from both asking questions directly and from observing his practices and intensity. I can't repeat enough how he could become so incredibly focused. The kitchen in our apartment was separated from his bedroom by the living room. When he was really focused on a writing project, he would occasionally take breaks and go into the kitchen to get a glass of water. On the way back to his room he'd stop to talk for a moment, and put his glass down. An hour or two later he'd repeat this, totally forgetting that he already had a glass of water. He'd get another glass and set it down. Soon there were glasses all over.

It didn't require me to be there for him to forget his glass. Sometimes, if I came home late at night, I'd have to be careful to walk through the maze he'd created by putting down half-empty glasses of water!

I remember, too, that one time I found him in the living room with hundreds of 3 × 5 cards on the floor. "What *are* you doing?" I asked. This was during a time before there were computer applications that would easily index a book, and he was going through the laborious task of making an index for one of his books *by hand*. This was an onerous, time-consuming task, but for a nonfiction book he felt it was necessary. He took a break and explained to me exactly what he was doing. It was from that lesson I learned how to manually index a book. The first edition of my *Modern Magick* was done that way, and I own my understanding of how to do it to Scott.

Scott truly "walked his talk." He had gone to a toy store and purchased several plastic toy monsters. Using magic, he transformed them into "guardians," talismans of protection for our apartment. I saw a news report that stated the area we lived in had one of the highest crime rates in all of San Diego. However, we never had any problem with crooks or burglars, even though we sometimes left doors or windows open and unlocked.

Perhaps the biggest worry we had was with the landlord. He was a fundamentalist Christian who also owned the business next door, a combination vacuum cleaner repair and gun shop! He would roll a large chalkboard covered with Christian messages in front of our apartment so people walking or driving buy could see it. Scott called our living there "hiding in plain sight."

Once, Scott told me he knew he would always die young. I told him that was nonsense. He turned out to be right.

Scott died on my birthday, March 28, in 1993. He was just 36. To this day I believe that as his illness worsened he chose March 28 to be welcomed into the Summerland—that place of peace, healing, and restoration before reincarnation—as his last joke on me. From that time on, whenever I had a birthday, I'd have to remember him.

He needn't have worried. I'll always remember my friend, Scott Cunningham.

Natural Magic

"In centuries past, when the nightmares we know of as cities had yet to be born, we lived in harmony with the earth and used her treasures wisely. Many knew the old magics of herbs and plants.

"Knowledge was passed down from one generation to another, and so the lore was widely circulated and used. Most country folk knew one herb that was a powerful protection against evil, or a certain flower that produced prophetic dreams, and perhaps a sure-fire love charm or two.

"Witches had their own intricate operations of herbal magic, as did the magicians and alchemists. Soon a body of magical knowledge accumulated surrounding the simple herbs that grew by fast-running streams, in verdant meadows, and high on lonely cliffs."

———

Thus begins the first chapter of Scott's *Magical Herbalism*, his first occult book. It tells us a lot about Scott's approach to living, magic, and writing that culminated this cycle of his life.

His writing style only appears basic. In actuality it's the mark of a trained writer seeking to share not just words and information, but also his vision, feelings, and spirit. His last sentence is filled with evocative language, allowing readers to see in their minds' eye fast-running streams, high and lonely cliffs, and verdant meadows, during a time which, as mentioned in the first paragraph, came before the "nightmares we know as cities."

Simple language, but it allows you to close your eyes and think of (or is it remember?) a time when brilliantly colored meadows went on for as far as you could see, while craggy, windswept cliffs revealed a rare herb that only a brave adventurer might grasp. I think this may have been what Scott dreamed of.

It's not remembered much now, but three decades ago there was a surprising amount of animosity between Pagans and ceremonial magicians. His mention of them together, assuming equality, matches what many feel today: neither path is superior, only different. But it was subversive for its time and, I believe, magically helped to decrease that tension.

Magical Herbalism begins with an introduction to what magic is: "the use of powers that reside within us and the natural objects of our world to cause change." Then, like today, many books are published that imply all you have to do is burn some herbs, wear a scent, or mumble some words and magic happens. If that were true, every book on magic would be locked up under the Patriot Act! Scott knew there was more to it and that it was the *combination* of our inner powers with natural objects that resulted in the magic.

The beginning of the book then goes into how to identify, gather, dry, and store magical herbs. This was practical advice from a practicing magical herbalist, as was the information on the tools you needed to do this kind of magic, all of which were easily made or obtained. Even the tools were magical, and Scott pointed out that their proper preparation for magical work was important.

Unlike some writers, this was not merely a repetition of information he had read. There were many times I'd come home to our apartment only to find bunches of herbs drying by hanging from the ceiling. Once, he decided to make "corn dollies," magical figures made of straw. He went into Mexico to get the straw, but it was of low quality. No matter how much he soaked it (in our bathtub!) the straw wouldn't get pliable enough to use. Eventually, he removed it (so we could get clean again), but he didn't throw the stalks out right away. There must have been some insect larvae in them because a few days later I opened the door to leave my room and was confronted with thousands of tiny moths! For days we had to shoo them out of the way just to watch some TV.

In the next section of the book, Scott goes into the magical uses of herbs for such topics as protection, divination, healing, and love. Here's a brief look at some of what he wrote:

Protection

Scott gives the following list as some of the most used protective herbs:

Angelica	Juniper
Asafoetida	Lady's Slipper
Ash twigs and leaves	Mistletoe
Avens	Mugwort
Balm of Gilead	Mullein
Basil	Peony Roots
Bay Laurel	Periwinkle
Betony	Pimpernel
Cyclamen	Rose Geranium
Dill	Rosemary
Elder berries or leaves	Rowan
Fennel	Rue
Fern	St. John's Wort
Flax	Snapdragon
Fumitory	Tarragon
Horehound	Trefoil
Hyssop	Vervain

Then he explains how to use some of them in making a protection sachet:

"Get a piece of white cotton cloth, seven inches square. Next, select three, seven, or nine of the dried herbs listed above. Take equal parts of each and place them into an earthenware bowl. Mix them together silently for a few moments with your hands and then set aside.

"Spread out the cloth on your altar. Transfer the herbs to the center of the cloth. Gather up the corners and, with a red piece of string, yarn, or thread, tie firmly around the gathered-up corners, capturing the herbs inside. As you tie the first knot, say in a firm voice:

I bind thee to protect this house and all within it.

"Knot twelve times more, repeating the above with each repetition. When finished, stand, facing north, holding aloft your magic knife in your strong hand, the sachet in the other. With the tip of the knife pressed against the sachet, say such words as these:

May this that I have fashioned tonight
Serve as guardian and protection for this house
And all who reside within it.
May it serve me well.

"If the sachet is being made for a car, boat, or other vehicle, substitute the proper words.

"Now, hang it up by its red thread, in the highest point of the house. If this is impossible, hang it inside a closet or over the main entrance.

"When used in cars or other vehicles, place it under the driver's seat. It is also good to make up a few extras to hang over the doorstep, or to bury in the garden. They are truly all-purpose devices."

Note that there are things you have to do to make this device work. Also note that Scott leaves a lot of room for individuality, allowing you to choose which herbs you want and that the invocation doesn't require you to use his exact words, only that you use "such words as these." You had to think about what you were doing, truly making these spells your own. This gave you knowledge, experience, and self-empowerment.

Scott was fascinated by scents, and the sections on scented oils, perfumes, and incenses hinted at his interest. In the following years aromatherapy became popular, and Scott communicated with some of the leaders in that field.

Divination

In this section, Scott first identifies the difference between divination, "the art of finding things out through the use of other than normal means," and clairvoyance, "the capability to *see clearly*, to be consciously psychic and be able to attain this state without the use of aids." The tools he suggests you can use include crystal balls, dowsing rods, pendulums, the Tarot, the I Ching, etc.

Scott then gives formulas for incenses, the scents of which can assist a person in performing divinations.

"**Witches' Sight Incense:** This is an all-purpose formula, to be burned while reading Tarot cards, using crystals, meditating, etc. It is composed of gum mastic, patchouli, cinnamon, juniper, and sandalwood.

"On a Wednesday, during the waxing Moon, take equal parts of the powdered herbs, mix well, and moisten with a few drops of mingled musk and ambergris oils. (The artificial ambergris will work; ambrette oil will do for the musk. If these are unavailable, use clove and nutmeg.)

"Mix until all particles are moistened, crumbly but not soggy. Let stand overnight, then pack in a jar, leaving the cork slightly loose.

"**Scrying Incense:** Many Witches employ crystal balls in their divination sessions. To strengthen the crystal, rub it with fresh mugwort leaves. While scrying (gazing), burn an incense composed of mugwort and wormwood, equal parts. Place the ball on the altar between two white candles, with the censer back on the other side of the ball."

Note, once again, the freedom that Scott allows the practitioner. He doesn't give exact amounts of the herbs, he gives relative amounts. That way you can make up small, medium, or large batches, whatever you can use. Scott doesn't give specific information on crystal ball scrying, either, but he does mention the concept of focus. The lights from the candles give a focal point within the crystal ball while the incense helps to open your psychic abilities. You may "see" images within the crystal, or the focusing may allow you to see them within your mind.

Healing

Since this book is on magical herbalism, Scott makes clear that he is not discussing the medicinal uses of herbs, but rather how herbs can be used magically to "cure, help speed recovery, and to prevent one from getting sick in the first place.

"The basis of magical healing is just that—magic. It uses the powers of herbs fortified and directed by the healer to heal the body directly through the force of magic."

Again in this section, Scott stresses that it is not just the mixing of herbs or burning of incenses that is important. Rather, it is the magic that *you* put into it. He writes, "Attitude is of the utmost importance. When preparing charms for yourself or for others, keep in your mind a vision of the person completely whole, healed and free of disease, injury, or whatever is the current problem. Negative thinking has no place in magic, so don't dwell on the illness or injury; forget it and concentrate on health and happiness."

Upon reading this, some people may believe that healing magic—in fact, *all* magic—is nothing but using your mind power. If that were true, it would make the use of herbs, spells, charms, wands, daggers, and the like unnecessary. However, it is *not* true. Rather, the use of the mind is just one aspect of the whole of magic. Flour is an important part of most cakes, but it is not the only thing that matters. You also may need such things as shortening, sugar, salt, baking powder, eggs, milk, and flavoring. You have to know how to put it all together, how to blend it, and exactly how much energy (baking) to give your mixture. Leave out any aspect and the cake will fail.

Similarly, with herb magic, you need to know how much of each herb (relative to the other herbs) to use, how to mix them, where your mind should focus, and how much magical energy you need to include.

Scott shares this recipe for healing incense:

"In a censor, burn a healing incense such as one composed of myrrh, rose buds, and saffron, ground together. Have a bowl of saffron water on the altar as well. To make saffron water, boil one pint of spring water. Add one tablespoon saffron. Cover with a cloth and let sit three minutes. Then strain the water through the cloth into a blue or crystal clear bowl. Set on the southern part of your altar.

"Wash your hands in the saffron water before actually beginning the rite, then dry your hands on a small cloth placed nearby for this purpose. Next, say a healing invocation to the deity you wish to invoke. A Witch who worshipped Isis might use something like the following:

Isis,
You who are all that ever was,
All that is,
And all that shall be,
Heal me as you healed Horus of all his wounds
Which Set, his brother, had inflicted on him.
O, Isis,
Great magician,
Heal me,
And deliver me from all fatal sicknesses,
Wounds,
And evil things,
And from diseases of every kind.

"Naturally, if using this invocation for another person, you would insert his or her name into the text in place of 'me.'"

Although many people think of Wicca as being simplistic, for people such as Scott, this was obviously not the case. Besides needing to know the basics of focusing the mind, energy work, the value of being positive (of success) in magic, and the knowledge of which herbs traditionally (and through personal work) can have a positive effect, Scott was also fascinated by mythology. In his invocation, he showed an understanding of ancient Egyptian mythology and how it can be applied to healing. I believe this should encourage all modern-day Pagans and other magical folk to increase their studies!

Scott continues to show his lack of dogmatism. He doesn't give a spell that you "must" use without changing a word. Rather, he shows by example and suggests that you create something just as he had done.

But burning incense was not the limit of Scott's instructions for magical healing. That is just what you burn while doing magical rites. He goes on to describe how to make healing amulets, techniques to magically help wounds heal, cure warts, overcome headaches, and even how to help ailing pets.

> *"When you or your patient is healthy again, make up a little sachet of dried rue and wear it at all times to avert disease."*

> *"Above all, live a balanced, healthy, and happy life."*

To me, that last sentence is very telling. One of the expressions I first presented in my book, *Modern Magick,* is:

> *Magick isn't something you do. Magick is something you are.*

Scott lived a magical life. To him, part of a magical life was being balanced, healthy, and happy. Part of that was using herbs magically. Oh, and he hated the use of the "k" in "magick." He always spelled the word "magic."

Love

Scott explains that "the herbs of love vibrate on a friendly and attracting plane. They set up an aura around the user that is irresistibly interesting and compelling." Although the concept seems to imply that you can use a spell to attract someone against his or her will, Scott considered this unethical. "Magicians and Witches never try to force anyone into love. [Such magic is] ... evil, as it attempts to control another person."

Unfortunately, Scott's ethics and idealism sometimes presented an unreal vision of the world. There are people who do evil things, and both magicians and Witches are people. It would be more accurate to say that *ethical* people, including magicians and Witches, would not use magic [or other means] to force someone into doing something against their will. True love magic makes you "irresistibly interesting and compelling" to someone who, consciously or unconsciously, is looking for love. It is a signal that you are available to those who are seeking.

"To attract a man, mix together [in a sachet] lavender, dried bachelor's buttons, and a tiny pinch of valerian root. Add a bay leaf and carry with you wherever you go."

I find this to be an interesting formula. It has sweet smells combined with the very earthy pitch of valerian (okay, valerian smells like used gym socks!). Many women's perfumes that use a combination of sweet and earthy scents are considered sexy. Perhaps the bay leaf brings out a note of delicious home cooking and is added because the "way to a man's heart is through his stomach."

Scott continues, "To attract a woman, [with a sachet] use patchouli, cinnamon, and henbane—(the latter traditionally gathered by the man in the morning, while standing naked on one foot!)."

The rest of the book consists of various recipes, formulas, and instructions on how to make an herb garden.

There are two other books that are important to note here. They are *Cunningham's Encyclopedia of Magical Herbs* and *Cunningham's Encyclopedia of Crystal, Gem & Metal Magic*. These two books have literally become major resources for every Pagan and Wiccan magical worker. They describe herbs, crystals, gems, etc., and give their magical uses.

There are basically two types of New Age, occult, or metaphysical shops. Some merely sell books and candles, stones, and herbs. They may have spell kits already made that you can use, but they don't prepare anything for you. The other type may have all of these things, but they also prepare specialized candles and herbal mixtures. I have traveled from Washington State to Florida, from New York to Hawaii. I always try to visit metaphysical shops. *Every* shop I've been to that prepares candles and herbs for users has one or both of Scott's encyclopedias behind the counter. They are usually beat-up and dog-eared from frequent use.

On occasion, Scott used to help out at Judith Wise's occult shop. Sometimes he would help with the oils. Judith would get oils in large bottles, and from those large bottles she would fill small vials and label them for sale. Once, while Scott was helping out, he was filling small vials with "Come to Me Lover" oil. He laughed when he told me that *somehow* some of the vials had a mistake on the labels. The word "to" had been replaced with "on." I'm sure he had nothing to do with that. *Right.*

The Goddess and Wicca

The Truth About Witchcraft booklet with its plain green cover was popular, but *The Truth About Witchcraft Today* (1988) started a subversive firestorm, beginning with its cover. There was no woman or man in flowing robes wearing lots of silver jewelry surrounded by censers, daggers, chalices, and pentagrams. The original cover showed a young woman in classy business attire. Strong and proud, she didn't need to broadcast her religion and beliefs with a costume of robes and silver. The cover on the latest edition also shows a young and successful woman, now in a pleasant home. And if these two women could be Witches, *anyone* could be a Witch!

In the introduction he describes a group of "robed figures, chanting in a long-dead language" who whirl around a table with candles. The motion stops and a woman calls on the God and Goddess to "Draw near us during this, our circle." It sounds like this could be an archetypical group of Witches, preparing to cast a spell.

But there is a bit of mental subversion in these words. For he reveals that this is taking place in an "upper-class home." Anyone, rich or poor, could be doing this. As Scott writes, "This is Witchcraft."

He then describes another scene, 2,000 miles away, where a fifteen-year-old girl fixes a green candle onto a photo of a friend. "In the darkened room she lights the candle. She closes her eyes: within her mind she visualizes a flowing purple light surrounding her boyfriend's broken arm. She chants an impassioned healing incantation.

"This, too, is Witchcraft."

Scott sees Witchcraft as being both a religion and a magical methodology. The magic practiced by Witches is folk magic. "Folk magic is just that—the magic of the people. Long ago, practicing simple magical rituals was as normal as eating or sleeping. Magic was a part of daily existence. To question its effectiveness, or indeed its necessity, was tantamount to a twentieth-century person questioning whether the Earth is round.

"Though times have changed, contemporary practitioners of folk magic accept the same principles and perform rituals similar to those of bygone eras.

"Folk magicians don't use supernatural powers. They're not out to control the world. They aren't dangerous or evil. They simply sense and utilize natural energies which have not yet been quantified, codified, and accepted into the hallowed halls of science.

"These energies spring from the Earth itself, not from demons or Satan. They're present within stones, colors, and herbs, as well as within our own bodies. Through timeless rituals, folk magicians rouse, release, and direct these energies for the purpose of creating positive, specific, needed change."

Scott goes on to say that these concepts will be foreign to the atheist, materialist, or Christian who has been taught to dominate and subdue the Earth, but not to the folk magicians. Folk magicians are persons who, unsatisfied by religious or physically based creeds, have investigated the Earth and its treasures. They've gone within themselves to sense the mystic powers of the human body and to feel its connections with the Earth.

"And they have discovered that magic works."

While Scott was trying to make a definition of people who were Witches and what they actually did, I think he was also—perhaps unconsciously—describing himself.

The book goes on to describe folk magic in greater detail, including its history, what spells are, the tools of a folk magician (crystals, colors, herbs, chants, etc.) and why "Harm None" is the simple universal source of an acceptable code of ethics, especially for the magician. When it comes to colors, he gives this list of their uses in magic:

White: Purification, protection, peace

Red: Protection, strength, health, courage, exorcism, passion

Black: Negation, absorption of disease and negativity

Blue: Healing, psychism, patience, happiness

Green: Finances, money, fertility, growth, employment

Yellow: Intelligence, theorization, divination

Brown: Healing (of animals), homes, housing

Pink: Love, friendships

Orange: Adaptability, stimulation, attraction

Purple: Power, healing (of severe disease), spirituality, meditation

———

"Candles," he writes, "are rubbed with fragrant oils and surrounded by crystals. Herbs may be piled up around their bases or scattered onto the working area. Various symbols could be scratched onto their surfaces...As the candle flames, the folk magician visualizes her or his need. The flame directs the personal power as well as that of the objects placed around it."

Scott writes that the vast majority of folk magicians work with positive, healing, and loving energy because:

- Magicians respect life

- Magicians respect the Earth

- Magicians respect the ultimate, universal force of power

• Power sent will be received in like kind

• Magic is love

Scott gives some examples of folk magic spells, including one for wealth called *A Silver Spell:*

"This ritual takes a week to perform.

"Situate a small bowl of any material in a place of prominence in your home, somewhere you pass by every day. Each day for seven days put one dime in the bowl.

"Next, obtain a green candle. This can be any shade of green [bought anywhere] ...

"Before you begin, fix in your mind the idea that you are a prosperous person. See money as being no problem. Imagine money coming to you as you need it.

"Place the bowl of dimes, the green candle, and a holder on a flat surface. Hold the candle in your hands and feel the power of money. Feel the avenues that open to you when you have it. Sense the energy within money which we as human beings have given to it. Place the candle in the holder. Pour the seven dimes into your left hand (or right hand if left-handed). You will create a circle surrounding the candle with the dimes. Place the first dime directly before the candle. As you place it say the following or similar words:

Money flow,
Money shine;
Money grow,
Money's mine.

"Repeat this six more times until you've created a circle around the candle with seven gleaming dimes.

"As you say the words and place the dimes, know that you're not just reciting and fooling around with pieces of metal. You're working with *power*—that which we've given money as well as that which is within yourself. Words too have energy, as does the breath on which they ride.

"When you've completed this, light the candle. Don't just flick a Bic lighter; strike a match and touch its tip to the wick. As it picks up the fire, sputters, melts, and rises to a shining flame, see money energy burning there. See the power of money flowing out from the seven dimes up to the candle's flame and then out to the atmosphere.

"Blow out the match, discard it in a heat-proof container, and settle down before the glowing candle and money. Sense the feeling of money in your life. Visualize (see with your mind's eye) a life filled with money to spare—a life in which bills are quickly paid and money will never again be a problem.

"See yourself wisely spending money, investing for your future needs. See money as an unavoidable and beautiful aspect of your life…

"After ten minutes or so, leave the area. Let the candle burn itself out in the holder (don't use a wooden one). Afterward, collect the dimes, place them back in the bowl, and 'feed' it a few coins every day from now on.

"Money will come to you."

Now in its fourteenth printing, *The Truth About Witchcraft Today* has sold over 150,000 copies.

The book is about more than just magic. It also covers the nature of Wicca, which Scott identified as the religion of the Witches. He writes,

"Folk magic is but half of what is termed Witchcraft. The other half is the religion known as Wicca. There are at least five major ways in which Wicca differs from other religions. These are:

- Worship of the Goddess and God

- Reverence for the Earth

- Acceptance of magic

- Acceptance of reincarnation

- Lack of proselytizing activities

Here, he notes that in "the recent past Wicca was primarily a secret initiatory religion." Again, this is a subtle and subversive introduction to change, implying that Wicca today need not be secret or initiatory. In a section on covens, he describes some as being "noninitiatory, arguing that human beings really have no right to initiate others. Others are self-initiatory, viewing this process as the domain of the Goddess and God." This book is an introduction and explanation of Witchcraft, so it really didn't include lots of spells and magical instructions. However, the sections he presented here opened the floodgates of what was to follow.

In *Wicca: A Guide for the Solitary Practitioner* (also 1988), Scott lays everything in the open.

> *"There is not, and can never be, one 'pure' or 'true' or 'genuine' form of Wicca. There are no central governing agencies, no physical leaders, no universally recognized prophets or messengers. Although specific, structured forms of Wicca certainly exist, they aren't in agreement regarding ritual, symbolism, and theology. Because of this healthy individualism, no one ritual or philosophical system has emerged to consume the others.*
>
> *"Wicca is varied and multifaceted. As in every religion,* **the Wiccan spiritual experience is one shared with deity alone.** *This book is simply one way, based on my experiences and the instruction I have received, to practice Wicca."* [Emphasis added]

And there, in the part I've made bold, is the secret. In Scott's opinion, Wicca—the religious aspect of Witchcraft—isn't about covens and secrets; it's about your personal spiritual experience with deity. You don't need a group. You don't need a (supposedly) ancient book or tradition. You just need the desire to establish a link with the Goddess and God.

Scott admits that most books on Wicca share similar views, "so most of the published Wiccan material is repetitive." Also, at the time he wrote the book, he stated that most Wiccan books "are geared toward coven (group) oriented Wicca. This poses a problem for anyone unable to find a minimum of four or five interested, compatible persons to create a coven. It also lays a burden on those who desire private religious practice."

The main part of the book begins with a section on theory covering the magic circle and altar, days of power, the tools of the Witch, ritual and preparation for ritual, and concludes with a section on initiation. In it, he asks, if "a person can be a

Wiccan only if she or he has received such an initiation [from another Wiccan] ... who initiated the first Wiccan?"

But Scott doesn't discard the notion of initiation, just its application. "True initiation isn't a rite performed by one human being upon another," he writes. "Initiation is a process, gradual or instantaneous, of the individual's attunement with the Goddess and God. Many of the Wicca readily admit that the ritual initiation is the outer form only. True initiation will often occur weeks or months later, or prior to, the physical ritual." He then states his radical, for the time, approach: "Rest assured, it's quite possible to experience a true Wiccan initiation without ever meeting another soul involved in the religion ... Some say, 'Only a Wiccan can make a Wiccan.' I say only the Goddess and God can make a Wiccan. Who's better qualified?"

With these words, Scott opened up Wicca to hundreds of thousands of people who were eagerly looking for a faith and a practice that came from their hearts and beliefs rather than ossified and codified books.

Of course, Scott talks about magic, too. "My latest, most refined definition [of magic] is: *Magic is the projection of natural energies to produce needed effects.*"

"*There are three main sources of this energy—personal power, earth power, and divine power.*

"**Personal power** *is the life force that sustains our earthly existences. It powers our bodies. We absorb energy from the moon and sun, from water and food. We release it during movement, exercise, sex, and childbirth. Even exhaling releases some power, though we recoup the loss through inhaling.*

"In magic, personal power is aroused, infused with a specific purpose, released, and directed toward its goal.

"**Earth power** *is that which resides within our planet and in its natural products. Stones, trees, wind, flames, water, crystals, and scents all possess unique, specific powers that can be used during a magical ritual.*

"A Wiccan may dip a quartz crystal in salt water to cleanse it and then press it against an ailing person's body to send its healing energies within. Or, herbs may be sprinkled around a candle that is burned to produce a specific magical effect. Oils are rubbed onto the body to effect internal changes.

"**Divine power** *is the manifestation of personal power and earth power. This is the energy that exists within the Goddess and God—the life force, the source of universal power that created everything in existence.*

"Wiccans invoke the Goddess and God to bless their magic with power. During ritual they may direct personal power to the deities, asking that a specific need be met. This is truly religious magic.

"And so, magic is a process in which Wiccans work in harmony with the universal power source that we envision as the Goddess and God, as well as with personal and earth energies, to improve our lives and to lend energy to Earth. Magic is a method whereby individuals under none but self-determined predestination take control of their lives."

The next section of the book describes how to design your own rituals, including a self-dedication. Scott also gives exercises and magical techniques, including journaling, breathing, visualization, and meditation. Here is one of his simple techniques to help improve your visualization abilities. This is valuable because *thoughts are things*. The implication of this is that magic occurs all the time. A powerful visualization for fifteen minutes to bring money into your life would have to "counteract twenty-three hours and forty-five minutes of daily, self-induced, negative programming. Thus we must keep our thoughts in order and in line with our desires and needs. Visualization can help here.

"Sit or lie comfortably with your eyes shut. Relax your body. Breathe deeply and still your mind. Pictures will continue to pop into your head. Choose one of these and stick with it. Let no images intrude other than the one you've chosen. Keep all thoughts revolving around the image. Retain this picture for as long as you can, then let it go and end the exercise."

Finally, Scott included many rituals and magical techniques. Here is an invocation that "may be chanted while moving or dancing around the altar to raise elemental energy for magical workings."

Invocation of the Elements

Air, fire, water, earth, elements of astral birth,
I call you now; attend to me!

In the circle, rightly cast,
safe from psychic curse or blast,
I call you now; attend to me!

From cave and desert, sea and hill,
by wand, blade, cup, and pentacle,
I call you now; attend to me!

This is my will, so mote it be!

Scott encouraged his readers to study the ancient deities. He would have encouraged you to find out everything possible about the God Pan in order to appropriately and effectively use the following invocation:

Invocation to Pan

O great God Pan,
beast and man,
shepherd of goats and lord of the land,

I call you to attend my rites
on this most magical of nights.

God of the wine,
God of the vine,
God of the fields and God of the kine,
attend my circle with your love
and send your blessings from above.

Help me to heal;
help me to feel;
help me to bring forth love and weal.
Pan of the forests, Pan of the glade,
be with me as my magic is made!

Numbers are important in rituals. Why use a certain number of candles or recite a chant a certain number of times? Scott gave this advice for designing rituals. "In general, odd numbers are related to women, receptive energy, and the Goddess; even numbers to men, projective energy, and the God." [Note: he did not include all numbers.]

- 1: The universe; The One; the source of all.

- 2: The Goddess and God; the perfect duality; projective and receptive energy; the couple; personal union with deity; interpenetration of the physical and spiritual; balance.

- 3: The triple Goddess; the lunar phases; the physical, mental, and spiritual aspects of our species.

- 4: The elements; the spirits of the stones; the winds; the seasons.

- 5: The senses; the pentagram; the elements plus akasha; a Goddess number.

- 7: The planets that the ancients knew; the time of the lunar phase; power; protection and magic.

- 8: The number of the sabbats; a number of the God.

- 9: A number of the Goddess.

- 13: The number of esbats; a fortunate number.

- 15: A number of good fortune.

- 21: The number of sabbats and moons in the Wiccan year; a number of the Goddess.

- 28: A number of the moon; a number of the Goddess.

- 101: The number of fertility.

The planets are numbered thus:

- Saturn: 3

- Jupiter: 4

- Mars: 5

- Sun: 6

- Venus: 7

- Mercury: 8

- Moon: 9

Scott notes that some people use different numerical systems and that this is simply the one he uses.

Scott follows with numerous recipes. Here are a few of his oil recipes:

Sabbat Oil No. 1

3 parts patchouli
2 parts musk
1 part carnation

Wear to the sabbats to promote communion with the deities.

Sabbat Oil No. 2

2 parts frankincense
1 part myrrh
1 part allspice
1 drop clove

Use as the above formula.

Full Moon Oil No. 1

3 parts rose
1 part jasmine
1 part sandalwood

Anoint the body prior to esbats (Full Moon rituals) to attune with lunar energies.

Full Moon Oil No. 2

3 parts sandalwood
2 parts lemon
1 part rose

Use as above.

And here are some of his spells.

Protective Chant

Visualize a triple circle of purplish light around your body while chanting:

> *I am protected by your might,*
> *O gracious Goddess, day and night.*

Another of the same type. Visualize a triple circle and chant:

> *Thrice around the circle's bound,*
> *evil sink into the ground.*

String Magic

"Take cord of the appropriate color, and shape it on the altar into a rune or the design of the object that you need: a car, a house, a paycheck, etc. While you do this, visualize the needed object; raise power and send it forth to bring it to manifestation. So shall it be."

———

Although it may seem odd to Wiccans and Witches today, the majority of whom regularly practice as solitaries, Scott— whose books were beloved and respected—actually writing a book saying it was okay to practice on your own and that you needn't be part of a coven really started a firestorm of controversy. This was so apparent that when Scott wrote his follow-up book, *Living Wicca,* he began with a note stating:

> *"This book, a further guide for solitary practitioners of Wicca, isn't an attack on conventional Wicca, Wiccan traditions, covens, or usual training procedures. It was written (as was its predecessor) for those without access to conventional Wicca, Wiccan traditions, covens, or usual training procedures.*
>
> *"Some will see this book as an insult to their form of Wicca, so I repeat: this is a guide for solitary practitioners who have no access to your form of Wicca. This in no way lessens it or any other Wiccan tradition."*

In *Wicca: A Guide for the Solitary Practitioner,* he had described the concepts and techniques of being a solitary Witch, including, of course, the magic of the Craft of the Wise. But to Scott, Wicca was not simply something to do between classes, after school or work, or on the weekend. For Scott, Wicca was something you lived every minute of the day. *Living Wicca* expands upon the concepts he introduced in his book *Wicca*. Here he takes you beyond simply *practicing* magic and various rituals and rites and moves you to *living* as a Wiccan and allowing the concepts of Wicca and Witchcraft to permeate everything you do.

Scott discusses challenges facing the new solitary Wiccan:

> "*Sometimes, however, reading more than a few books may lead to confusion. Authors may make contradictory statements regarding Wiccan ritual practices and concepts. Some may deliberately obscure Wiccan knowledge with mystic prose. The solitary Wiccan, grasping for answers, may only come up with more questions, as expert after expert states that her or his way is the best or most effective…*
>
> "*One book may state, 'the altar is always in the east'; in another, the north. An author might write that counterclockwise movement within the circle is forbidden; another will direct the reader to move in precisely this direction. Dates and names for the sabbats and esbats vary widely according to the author. Tools are given differing names, attributes, and functions.*
>
> "*Eventually, the books that originally inspired the new solitary Wiccan may become a source of confusion and despair, and she or he may pack them away, deciding that no real learning can be achieved with them.*
>
> "*This is a shame, and can be avoided by keeping this concept in mind: Each book is a different teacher. Each teacher has distinct ideas concerning the subject being taught. Think of four experienced race-car drivers who are teaching beginners. Each instructs his or her student in the basics of this dangerous sport. The fastest engine designs; the best oil; the*

> *most effective strategy to use during the races themselves. Each driver teaches this subject in a different way, and expresses her or his biases, but they're all teaching racing.*
>
> *"Wiccan books, as teachers, are quite similar. Experience and training have created specific ideals concerning Wicca within each book's writer, and these ideals are clearly presented within her or his books. Divergences of opinion are natural in experts in any field and shouldn't dismay those who are confronted by them."*

"When you're challenged with seemingly contradictory information, examine this information and make a decision as to which to follow. Listen to your intuition. In other words, feel free to pick and choose among the published rituals and ritual textbooks to decide what *feels* right. It's this selectivity that will usually prove to be the most effective."

Once again, Scott was being subversive. Instead of demanding that you had to follow whatever the coven and its leader said, he advised that the ultimate authority had to be you and your relationship to the Goddess and God. If it works for you, use it. If it doesn't work, discard it. In this way, Wicca became truly yours and not someone else's beliefs. Similarly, the beliefs and practices of others are theirs and are just as legitimate as yours.

During the early years of Wicca, there were interminable "Witch Wars," battles between covens and traditions as to which ones were "real" or "legitimate." With the above comments, Scott worked his magic to literally end most of the Witch Wars. Those that remain tend to be limited to whether or not one coven legitimately came out of another and whether a person is working following some basic Wiccan concepts such as the Wiccan Rede of "An it harm none, do what ye will." [Note: In the usage here, "An" is an Old English word for "If."]

So how should someone make Wicca part of his or her life? Scott suggests you begin in four ways:

- *Study* everything you can.

- *Think* about everything you study and learn, and come to your own conclusions.

- If things don't make sense, *pray* to the Goddess and God for guidance.

- *Experiment.* Put what you've learned, including magic, into practice. If it works, keep it; if it doesn't work, use something else.

The book continues with advice for approaching life from a Wiccan point of view, including what happens when you are ill and how to deal with it. He points out ways to select a magical name and then gives a self-initiation into Wicca ritual. Sort of.

Unlike most books, he doesn't spell out exactly what to say and do in such a ritual. Rather, he gives you the concepts of what should be covered and lets you fill it in, making it as simple or complex as you desire and letting you choose the words and deities. Here's what he writes should be included in a self-initiation:

- Purification of some kind. (A shower or bath is fine.)

- The laying of the altar. (Use whatever tools you normally work with.)

- The circle casting. (Though this isn't absolutely necessary, it certainly heightens the atmosphere. It's best if you've already gained proficiency in circle casting before initiation. If you feel comfortable casting the circle, use it. If not, don't.)

- Opening invocations to the Goddess and the God. (These may be those that you use in your everyday Wiccan ritual work, or special ones composed for this rite.)

- A symbolic death of your old, non-Wiccan self. (Be creative. This may consist of wrapping yourself in black cloth; blindfolding yourself while sitting before the altar [not while walking]; even singing a dirge. Create a prayer appropriate for this moment. After a suitable time of meditation and reflection, cast off the trappings of death with a cry of joy.)

- Pray anew to the Goddess and God, dedicating yourself to them. State that you're now a Wiccan. If you've chosen a magical name, say it aloud: "I [your magical name], am now a Wiccan" would be a suitable formula for inclusion in your dedicatory prayer.

- Relax in the circle for a few minutes. Watch the candle's flames. If you've brought cakes and wine into the circle, it's time to dedicate them and to share in the manifested love of the Goddess and God. When you've finished your sacred meal, thank the Goddess and God for their attendance and close the circle.

Scott includes a chapter on how the concepts of Wicca relate to everyday life. These include harming none, reincarnation, karma, magic, thought, Earth stewardship (caring for our planet), and experiencing the continuous presence of the Goddess and God. He shows how these concepts are applicable at work, school, and in the home. He encourages you to make an offering to the Goddess and God each day and describes the secrets of effective prayer to them, including the realization that our bodies are sacred and that the Goddess and God are within us as well as outside of us. "They don't reside in any one part of us; they're simply within. They exist within our DNA. They're present in our souls. The Goddess and God are infused into every aspect of our beings."

Scott gives directions for how to design your own prayers and magical rites, and then gives the key to the future of Wicca: how to design your own tradition.

Together, *Wicca: A Guide for the Solitary Practitioner* and *Living Wicca* are the basis for the magic that has created one of the fastest-growing religions in the world today. They are two of the most important and vital books for Wiccans, Witches, and Pagans around the world.

The Magic of Hawaii

In support of my own published writings, along with incredible good fortune, I have traveled all over the United States and into Europe giving workshops and lectures. In the continental United States, I have been to most states, from California to New York, from Washington State to Florida. Each state has its own unique qualities and style.

But there is nothing like Hawaii.

Everything from the friendliness of the indigenous people to the massive and fragrant flowers is unique to Hawaii. Where else on earth do the favorite foods include the canned meat known as Spam (served at McDonald's and Burger King!) and a type of snow cone called "shave ice" (usually spelled "shaved ice" but pronounced "shave")?

I have been to Kona three times. On those occasions, Kona —a *moku* or district on the western coast of the island of Hawaii—was hot and humid. I asked a taxi driver what he'd do if it got too hot and muggy. "We just stop for awhile and go for a swim in the ocean," he replied, sharing a common relaxed (but definitely *not* lazy) spirit. A common Hawaiian hand sign is known as the *shaka*. It is made by making a fist and extending the thumb and pinky while rotating the hand back and forth at the wrist. It means things like "hello," "goodbye," "hang loose," "see you later," etc. Even between various ethnic cultures that might normally disagree, the *shaka* is understood to represent the *aloha spirit* of friendship and understanding.

The hundreds of islands, including the eight major islands, in the chain that forms Hawaii weren't known to Europeans until 1778. Explorers, traders, and whalers found Hawaii's harbors helpful. First they came as visitors. Then, as seems to have been a practice of the times, as conquerors. Missionaries converted the people from the local beliefs. An alliance of British and U.S. troops landed in 1874 and forced a government on the people, stripping most natives of the vote and taking away any power from the ruling queen, Lili'uokalani. She tried to re-establish her government, but the wealthy and powerful foreigners prevented it. It was only in 1993 that the U.S. government apologized for the overthrow of the lawful Hawaiian Kingdom.

In 1898 Hawaii was annexed, becoming a U.S. territory. It was granted self-rule in 1900. Real power, however, was in the hands of a group of five wealthy plantation owners, and for them there were advantages to keeping Hawaii a territory. In 1950, their hold over the Islands was broken, and less than a decade later, Hawaii became the fiftieth state of the United States.

The influence of Christianity had decimated local beliefs, much as it had in Europe. In Europe, Christianity ruled for over 1,500 years and to this day Pagan beliefs and practices still exist. Although some Christians tried to wipe out local beliefs in Hawaii (native religion, language, and even the hula dance were outlawed), the control of Christianity over the Islands was much briefer. To protect their beliefs, little of that inner knowledge was shared with non-natives. As programs to promote native Hawaiian culture now appear, this taboo against sharing with outsiders is slowly breaking down.

But it was only at the beginning of this breakdown when Scott first started visiting Hawaii. He told me that although he could learn some of the native spiritual beliefs and magic, the innermost initiatory secrets were kept from the *haoles* (people not born on the islands; foreigners). I believe he was truly saddened by this exclusion.

In the late 1980s and early 1990s, when Scott was traveling frequently to Hawaii, there were a few popular books available that were supposedly about Hawaiian magic. Most were just retreads and imaginative expansions of Max Freedom Long's 1948 book *The Secret Science Behind Miracles*. Although Long spent time in Hawaii, he was also a "New Thought" (precursor to New Age) philosopher, and much of what he wrote was New Thought disguised as Hawaiian spirituality. Since so many have copied him, the validity of much of what was popularly called Hawaiian magic and spirituality is questionable.

And this, again, is one of the reasons I have so much respect for Scott. He did intensive research in Hawaii from original sources. His book (originally published in 1994 as *Hawaiian Religion and Magic,* followed by a second edition, *Hawaiian Magic and Spirituality,* in 2000 and now published as *Cunningham's Guide to Hawaiian Magic & Spirituality*) is so well researched that I believe it could be a textbook for a college anthropology class. Even so, it's written in Scott's distinctive style so that anyone can understand it and even use many of the concepts and techniques as part of their spiritual and magical practices.

Scott's attraction to Hawaii was deep and very personal. The amazing flowers and plants that are there are natively found nowhere else in the United States. This was bound to attract the interest of anyone as focused on herbs and scents as Scott. But there was more.

Scott was a seeker. His research was an example of his need to discover new things. I believe he was really looking for a spiritual tradition that was both ancient and traditional and not a blend of some ancient ideas with modern ones. I think he found this in Hawaii.

Ignoring Long and his copyists, Scott's research led him to a spiritual and magical system that was truly ancient and Pagan. He saw in it a continuous line of spirituality that even had similarities with the pre-Celtic traditions of the British Isles. No, I'm not suggesting that there were necessarily communications and direct links. Rather, there were practices by both the ancient peoples of Hawaii and of Great Britain that resulted in similar approaches to the Divine, to life, to the world, and to magic.

Scott loved the Hawaiian goddess Pele and the mountain that bears her name. He told me stories of the *Menehune*, the Hawaiian mystical little people, just as he had earlier told me about the way some people saw the ancient Picts as a type of little people. As an astrological Water sign (Cancer), of course Scott would love the Islands. They would be like a home to him as surely as if he had grown up there. Perhaps he did so in a past life. Perhaps the feeling that the islands were his true home kept drawing him back.

The U.S. education system and the way it presents history has been highly Eurocentric. The study of ancient history generally focuses on Greece and Rome. We learn little of the vast empires in China or the growth of massive civilizations in India. It's no wonder, then, that most Westerners know little or nothing of the history of Hawaii and its indigenous culture. To remedy this, Scott's book begins by discussing the history of Hawaii as well as the spiritual beliefs of the people, including the deities. He explains the major gods: Kane, Ku, Lono, and Kanaloa—and goddesses: Haumea, Hina, Laka, Ka'ahupahau, and Hi'iaka. He also examines numerous minor deities and the special place of Pele, as well as ancestor worship.

Scott then examines the nature of magic among traditional Hawaiians. He looks at the natural magical power, known as *mana*. "All *mana*," Scott writes, "originates with the deities." Some people have more or less of this nonphysical energy. "There were two types of *mana*: that with which humans are born and that which was acquired." He describes how it was considered possible to transfer *mana* from one person to another, lose your *mana* through misuse of skills, find different types of *mana* in different objects, and the special *mana* of women.

Scott next describes traditional types of *kapu* or taboos. Women, for example, were forbidden to cook food for themselves or to touch men's fishing equipment. Certain fish and fishing areas were limited to protect them for future generations. Seaweed, seen as food for fish, was also protected. Thus, the early Hawaiians were some of the first conservationists. There were also various taboos concerning everything from clothes to sleeping arrangements. For a time, breaking even minor taboos could result in severe punishments.

The book continues with a discussion of things important to the Hawaiians, including water, stones, rain, salt water, colors, plants, and the special dance, the *hula*. Today, the *hula* is presented as entertainment, but earlier it was sacred and people had to be very dedicated to go through the extensive training required to learn it. From 1830–1874, Christians had the *hula* banned as part of forbidding traditional Hawaiian spirituality.

Finally, this section discusses the *Menehune*, the Hawaiian version of pixies and brownies, as well as the traditional beliefs surrounding ghosts. With this Scott leaves his examination of the spirituality and beliefs of the Hawaiians and moves on to *ho'okalakupua*: magic.

"Hawaiians apparently didn't see magic as a supernatural practice. On the contrary, since it was performed with the use of mana, which resided within all animate and inanimate things, they probably couldn't have conceived of its use as being contrary to the laws of nature. Indeed, magic was

the use of the spiritual power that is resident within nature. Apparently, any use of mana to create wondrous change was an act of magic.

"Hawaiian magic," Scott continues, "was fairly simple in its organization and theories. Three things were necessary: the mana of the individual performing the rite, the mana of those objects used, and the pule (prayer) uttered. The prayer could be both the trigger and the release mechanism of the mana."

Love magic seems to have been popular. In one example, Scott describes how a "love expert" (*kahuna aloha*) prayed over a particular type of sugar cane, dedicating the magic to *Makanikeoe*, the god of the winds. The person who had consulted with the love expert would then "eat the cane and blow in the direction of the beloved. The wind god carried the love *mana* to the desired person. Once touched by it, she or he was suffused with love."

For excellence in *hula*, a graduate of a *hula* school would offer a goatfish with a prayer.

For success in all undertakings, a rock-clinging fish known as the *napili* (*nopili* on the island of Kauai) was prepared while praying and then offered to the gods so that success would cling to the practitioner.

A flat, water-polished black stone was placed under the pillow for safe, restful sleep.

Scott also includes information on the beliefs in omens, divination methods, and spirit possession.

Conclusion

As I write this, it's been almost nineteen years since Scott left for the Summerland. I still miss him. I hope I've been able to share with you some insights into who Scott was, what he was like, and the beliefs and feelings that drew him to his path. I also hope you've seen a glimpse of Scott's magical techniques, his own spiritual development, and the rather astounding magic Scott performed on the world. It's rare that one person can positively affect so many lives and help change what was a relatively small, almost cloistered faith into a massively growing world religion. One form of Scott's magic—his writing—accomplished this amazing feat.

There is another form of magic that Scott brought out in people. I see it in people's faces when they talk about Scott's books and his ideas. It's something undeniable: there is love in their hearts. I know this for a fact because it's the same look I have when I think about him.

But it's not just love for Scott. It's also love in the heart for the Goddess and God, for a spiritual path, and for others. Perhaps that's the ultimate form of magic Scott brought to hundreds of thousands of people.

Because love is the greatest magic of all.